# Social Media Marketing Social Media Marketing and Ads to Grow and Monetize Your Personal Brand in 2019

*How To Avoid Beginner Mistakes and Hack Your Facebook, Instagram, Youtube, LinkedIn and Ads for Massive Growth and Profit*

**A. STEEL**

© **Copyright 2019 - All rights reserved.**

The content contained within this book may not be reproduced, duplicated or transmitted without direct written permission from the author or the publisher.

Under no circumstances will any blame or legal responsibility be held against the publisher, or author, for any damages, reparation, or monetary loss due to the information contained within this book. Either directly or indirectly.

Legal Notice:

This book is copyright protected. This book is only for personal use. You cannot amend, distribute, sell, use, quote or paraphrase any part, or the content within this book, without the consent of the author or publisher.

Disclaimer Notice:

Please note the information contained within this document is for educational and entertainment purposes only. All effort has been executed to present accurate, up to date, and reliable, complete information. No warranties of any kind are declared or implied. Readers acknowledge that the author is not engaging in the rendering of legal, financial, medical or professional advice. The content within this book has been derived from various sources. Please consult a licensed professional before attempting any techniques outlined in this book.

By reading this document, the reader agrees that under no circumstances is the author responsible for any losses, direct or indirect, which are incurred as a result of the use of information contained within this document, including, but not limited to, — errors, omissions, or inaccuracies.

# Table of Contents

INTRODUCTION .................................................................................................. 8

**SECTION 1: THE FOUNDATION OF YOUR PERSONAL BRAND** .......................... 10

**CHAPTER 1 - WHAT IS A PERSONAL BRAND?** ................................................ 10

    10 ELEMENTS THAT CAN HELP TO BUILD A STRONG PLATFORM FOR PERSONAL BRANDING ............................................................................................................................. 11
    HISTORY OF PERSONAL BRANDING .......................................................................... 14
    7 PERSONAL BRAND ARCHETYPES ........................................................................... 16
    ARE YOU CAPABLE OF BECOMING AN INFLUENCER IN YOUR OWN NICHE? ..................... 19
    DO YOU HAVE THE CAPABILITIES TO PROMOTE YOUR OWN PRODUCTS? ........................ 19
    CONSIDER PROMOTING PRODUCTS THROUGH AFFILIATE MARKETING ............................ 21
    WHAT ARE YOUR BRAND VALUES? .......................................................................... 21
    IMPORTANCE OF CONNECTION, AUTHORITY, AND TRUST WHEN PROMOTING PRODUCTS . 22
    IMPORTANT FACTORS TO CONSIDER TO TRULY CONNECT WITH YOUR AUDIENCE ............. 23

**CHAPTER 2 - TRADITIONAL VERSUS MODERN MARKETING** ........................... 25

    DIFFERENT FORMS OF TRADITIONAL MARKETING ....................................................... 25
    MODERN METHODS OF MARKETING ........................................................................ 27
    THE INTERACTIVE QUALITIES OF SOCIAL MEDIA MARKETING ....................................... 28
    BENEFITS OF HAVING A SOCIAL MEDIA COMMUNITY ................................................... 31
    TIPS TO BUILD A STRONG SOCIAL MEDIA COMMUNITY ............................................... 33
    THINGS TO AVOID WHEN BUILDING A SOCIAL MEDIA COMMUNITY ............................... 34

**CHAPTER 3 - TARGET AUDIENCE AND MESSAGE** ............................................ 36

    HOW TO FIND YOUR AUDIENCE ON SOCIAL MEDIA .................................................... 36
    IDENTIFYING YOUR AUDIENCE ................................................................................ 37
    SURVEY EXISTING CUSTOMERS ............................................................................... 37
    FIND YOUR TARGET AUDIENCE IN FACEBOOK GROUPS ............................................... 38

TAILOR YOUR CONTENT BASED ON YOUR TARGET AUDIENCE ........................................38
PUT UP PERSONAL AND REAL CONTENT ..................................................................39
SENDING OUT A MESSAGE TO FOLLOWERS AND TARGET AUDIENCES ..........................40
CREATE CONTENT THAT IS IN SYNC WITH YOUR BRAND VALUES ................................40
ENSURE YOUR PERSONAL BRANDING STRATEGY IS APPROPRIATE ...............................41
HOW TO SEND A MESSAGE TO YOUR TARGET AUDIENCE ............................................43
THINGS TO AVOID WHEN SENDING A MESSAGE TO YOUR TARGET AUDIENCE .................44

## CHAPTER 4 – HOW TO MONETIZE YOUR PERSONAL BRAND .......................... 46

AWARENESS PHASE ..............................................................................................46
INTEREST PHASE ...................................................................................................46
EVALUATION PHASE ..............................................................................................47
DECISION PHASE ...................................................................................................47
PURCHASE PHASE .................................................................................................48
PERSONAL BRANDING AND THE SALES FUNNEL .......................................................48
WHAT INFLUENCES BUYER PURCHASE BEHAVIOR? ...................................................49
PURCHASING POWER ............................................................................................49
GROUP INFLUENCE ................................................................................................50
MARKETING AND ADVERTISING CAMPAIGNS ............................................................50
PERSONAL PREFERENCES .......................................................................................51
A NEED FOR VALIDATION .......................................................................................51
DECISION ANXIETY/CUSTOMER OBJECTIONS ............................................................52
THE "SPECIAL" CUSTOMER ....................................................................................52
THE "ME FIRST" CUSTOMER ..................................................................................53
THE SHOPAHOLIC ..................................................................................................53

## SECTION 2: BUILDING YOUR PERSONAL BRAND ........................................... 56

## CHAPTER 5 - OVERVIEW OF DIFFERENT CHANNELS ....................................... 56

FACEBOOK ...........................................................................................................56
INSTAGRAM ..........................................................................................................59
YOUTUBE .............................................................................................................61
LINKEDIN .............................................................................................................63
UNDERSTAND YOUR CUSTOMER .............................................................................65
UNDERSTANDING EACH SOCIAL MEDIA PLATFORM ...................................................65
SOCIAL MEDIA TO BUILD YOUR PERSONAL BRAND ...................................................67
FIND THE RIGHT GROUPS .......................................................................................67

- Keep Your Image Consistent .................................................................. 68
- Engage Regularly ..................................................................................... 68
- Diversify Your Content ............................................................................ 69
- Study Influencers .................................................................................... 69
- Ask Questions ......................................................................................... 70
- Jump into Discussions ............................................................................. 70
- Monitor Your Name ................................................................................ 71

## CHAPTER 6 - FACEBOOK MARKETING AND ADVERTISING ............................ 72

- Define Your Business .............................................................................. 73
- Learn Who Your Followers and Fans Are ................................................ 73
- Choose a Good Strategy .......................................................................... 74
- Turn Off Tagging ..................................................................................... 74
- Create a Vanity URL ................................................................................ 75
- Post Updates ........................................................................................... 75
- Link Your Facebook Page to Other Social Media Pages ........................... 76
- Use Events to Your Advantage ................................................................ 76
- Components of a Facebook Advertisement ............................................ 77
- The Importance of the Right Design ....................................................... 79
- Targeting the Right Audience ................................................................. 79
- Goal of Facebook Marketing ................................................................... 80
- Building a Brand in The Community ....................................................... 80
- Customer Service .................................................................................... 80
- Fan Page ................................................................................................. 81
- Social Media Mistakes to Avoid on Facebook ......................................... 81
- Creating Fun Social Media Posts ............................................................. 88
- Promote Your Facebook Business Page for Free ..................................... 91
- Facebook Advertisements and Small Startups ........................................ 93
- Increase Facebook Engagement ............................................................. 95
- Posting the Right Amount of Times ........................................................ 96
- Post When They Are Online .................................................................... 96
- Create Advertisements Specifically for Facebook ................................... 97
- Experiment with Videos .......................................................................... 97
- Interact with People ................................................................................ 97
- Get Creative ............................................................................................ 99
- Lookalike of The Existing Leads .............................................................. 99
- Instructions on How to Use the Facebook Ad Manager ........................ 100

- STEP-BY-STEP GUIDE TO CREATE FACEBOOK ADVERTISEMENTS .................. 101
- MEASURE AND REPORT ................................................................. 103
- HOW TO ADVERTISE MORE EFFECTIVELY ........................................... 104

## CHAPTER 7 - INSTAGRAM MARKETING AND ADVERTISING ...................... 111

- SET IT UP THE RIGHT WAY ............................................................. 111
- STORIES ARE GREAT ..................................................................... 112
- CHECK OUT THE LATEST TRENDS ..................................................... 112
- REPLY TO COMMENTS REGULARLY ................................................... 112
- INFLUENCER MARKETING ............................................................... 113
- GET FAMILIAR WITH HASHTAGS ...................................................... 113
- INFLUENCERS VS PAID ADVERTISEMENTS VS NON-PAID PROMOTIONS ......... 114
- INSTAGRAM VIDEOS & PHOTOS VS FACEBOOK VIDEOS & PHOTOS .............. 116
- IDEAL LENGTH OF INSTAGRAM VIDEOS ............................................. 117
- MISTAKES BEGINNERS MAKE WHILE ADVERTISING ON INSTAGRAM ............ 121

## CHAPTER 8 - YOUTUBE MARKETING AND ADVERTISING ......................... 124

- YOUTUBE MARKETING STRATEGIES .................................................. 125
- KINDS OF VIDEOS YOU CAN CREATE ON YOUTUBE ............................... 125
- TOOLS FOR VIDEO CONTENT .......................................................... 127
- TIPS FOR INCREASING SUBSCRIBERS AND VIEWS ................................ 127
- INCREASE TRAFFIC TO YOUR YOUTUBE VIDEOS ................................... 128

## CHAPTER 9 - LINKEDIN MARKETING ................................................... 131

- THE PROS AND CONS OF LINKEDIN MARKETING .................................. 132
- THE PROS & CONS OF USING VIDEO ON LINKEDIN ............................... 134
- TIPS FOR ATTRACTING FOLLOWERS ON LINKEDIN ................................ 136
- MISTAKES THAT ARE KILLING YOUR LINKEDIN PROFILE ......................... 137

## CHAPTER 10 - OTHER MARKETING CHANNELS ..................................... 140

- TWITTER ................................................................................... 140
- SNAPCHAT ................................................................................. 141
- PINTEREST ................................................................................ 141
- BLOGGING AND SEO .................................................................... 141

## SECTION 3: MONETIZING AND GROWING YOUR PERSONAL BRAND ............ 143

## CHAPTER 11 – BUILDING AN EMAIL LIST ............................................ 143

- Using Lead Magnets to Your Advantage ............................................................ 144
- Send Leads Through a Sales Funnel ................................................................. 145

## CHAPTER 12 - GROWTH AND MONETIZATION ............................................. 146

- Ways to Make Your Content Marketing Go Viral ............................................. 147
- Study Influencers .................................................................................................. 148
- Tips on Monetizing Your Personal Brand ........................................................ 149
- What Not to Do If You Want to Monetize Your Personal Brand ................... 150

## CONCLUSION ............................................................................................................. 152

# Introduction

Technology is evolving with each passing day, and in order for business owners to stay at the top of their game, it is important for them to make the right decisions. It's no secret that without having an internet presence, businesses will find it tough to survive. In order for your business to grow and become successful, you need to follow the right methods of promotion and marketing. With the world addicted to social media, social media platforms are the best place to garner attention and get more customers interested in your business.

Social media marketing has become one of the most popular forms of marketing in recent years. It is an affordable and effective method of marketing that helps business owners attract customers and create an online brand.

Social media marketing also helps to increase the number of visitors on a website which works in favor of various SEO purposes. Apart from being able to garner more attention and increase your customer base, you also become more visible on search engines which helps to get repeat business.

Social media marketing also manages to deliver higher conversion rates in comparison to most online marketing methods. While email marketing manages to generate around a 4-5% conversion rate, the rates of conversion with social media marketing are almost as high, making it a great alternative to email marketing which has a limited audience to advertise to based on your email list. You can increase the odds by marketing your business on social media in a unique method that catches people's attention.

Social media marketing is a transparent method of marketing that opens the doors to two-way communication. This is a great option for anyone who wants to stay loyal to one brand long-term. It gains the trust of customers and lets people know that the quality of your products and services are good - this improves brand loyalty to a great extent.

Social media marketing was first introduced as an alternative to advertising on various search engines. It has now become the mainstream method of marketing for a number of businesses. A staggering 82%[1] of small businesses and entrepreneurs have shifted focus to social media marketing for a reason.

If you want to make social media marketing part of your regular marketing strategy, then it's important you get it right. When you use social media marketing to your advantage, you will not only manage to increase the visibility of your business by almost 13%[2] on average, but you will establish a personal brand. This book will guide you through the various stages of social media marketing and the required steps you need to take on different platforms to increase your presence and let people know about your business and your brand.

---

[1] https://lookinla.com/2018/08/23/10-ways-social-media-marketing-can-help-grow-your-business/
[2] https://lookinla.com/2018/08/23/10-ways-social-media-marketing-can-help-grow-your-business/

# Section 1: The Foundation of Your Personal Brand

## Chapter 1 - What is A Personal Brand?

Personal branding is a process wherein individuals undertake certain steps that are required to market their brands and themselves. Personal branding is an operation of creating a specific impression or idea in the minds of groups, individuals, or organizations. In the concept of personal branding, an individual often uses his or her own name to create a brand image of the products that are being marketed.

One such commonly known example of personal branding is that of President Donald Trump, using his own name on all the buildings that his company has constructed. Another popular example is Kim Kardashian's use of her personal brand to endorse products. Her powerful and influential image plays a profound role in creating a massive demand in the market for products she personally advocates.

# 10 Elements That Can Help to Build a Strong Platform for Personal Branding

### *Personality Plays a Crucial Role*

Having a powerful and impactful personality is essential for one to build a strong foundation for a personal brand. Write down a list of your most profound features and traits and learn how to use these traits in your favor. For instance, if you have a funny and quirky personality, you may be the perfect personal brand ambassador for products that have an eccentric vibe to them. On the other hand, if you have an intellectual and tech-savvy personality, you can probably endorse technological products like smartphone and laptops. Before you start your personal branding career, figure out the strengths and weaknesses of your personality and work in sync with your strengths.

### *Your Values Matter*

The principles on which you operate, qualify as your values. You need to make sure that you maintain your principles and values for your personal branding and when you are endorsing a particular product. When you're in sync with the values that you deem most importance to you, you will automatically be more confident, energetic, and more alluring to others.

*Interest and Passion*

You need to know and understand the things that you're passionate about and deeply interested in. The things that you're passionate about will be a strong source of motivation for you and they should be used to lay down a foundation for your personal brand. When an individual is deeply passionate about something, it makes his or her personality mesmerizing to others. Hence, it is important that you figure out your passion and weave that into your personal branding.

*Make Full Use of Your Strengths*

You need to be aware of and make full use of all your strengths if you want to lay down a solid foundation for personal branding. Your body language, your communication skills, your digital communication skills, your style, and other strengths can play a vital role in helping you build a powerful personal brand.

*Education and Knowledge*

You never know when your prior education will have a profound impact on your personal branding. The knowledge and skills that you have gathered through the course of your life can prove to be very useful when you are endorsing a product through personal branding.

## Inspiration and Motivation

If you want to have a strong and impactful personal brand that motivates and inspires others, you need to have your very own source of inspiration and motivation yourself. Whether it is your college professor or a successful billionaire whose footsteps you wish to follow, it is recommended that you jot down the qualities and achievements of your mentor and strive to achieve these yourself.

## Your Style

Your way of dressing, your hairstyle, and demeanor all play a very important role in personal branding. You need to sport a style that screams "YOU" in that people are able to identify with you. Your uniqueness will have a direct impact on your personal brand.

## Goals

Once you have completely understood and figured out yourself and your personality, your next step is all about setting goals of where you want to be in the short-term and long-term. It is very important to set goals if you wish to successfully build and grow your personal brand.

## Target Market

You need to figure out which companies, individuals,

stakeholders, and businesses are most likely to be in your target market. Your target market is defined as the people or organizations whose attention you will capture in order to grow successfully as a personal brand. All the messages that you are putting out in the corporate world will be tailored to suit your target market.

### Connections

Last but not least, the connections that you maintain have a powerful impact on your personal brand. If you are connected to important, successful, or famous people, your brand too will become well-recognized and successful. So make sure that you always interact and build relationships with people who can and will have a positive impact on your personal brand.

Now that you know and understand all about the basics of personal branding and the 10 important elements that have a direct impact on the foundation of your personal brand, the next step is to learn all about the history of personal branding.

# History of Personal Branding

The concept of personal branding was first introduced in 1937 in a book that was written by Napoleon Hill. The book "Think and Grow Rich" incepted the idea of personal branding in the minds of business owners across the globe. Following his basic idea and concept, another famous writer by the name of Tom Peters emphasized personal branding in his article "The Brand

Called You". This article promoted the idea of self-branding and it brought about a major shift in the business and marketing worlds. With the introduction of the internet, the entire notion of personal branding shot through the roof. More and more business owners and celebrities began to maintain a specific online identity or personal brand with the sole intention of being able to affect and influence the real world. Before you begin to set down the foundation of your own personal brand, it is essential that you understand the primary goal of your brand. There are seven different personal brand archetypes. You need to properly understand each these archetypes and figure out which one best fits your style and personality.

# 7 Personal Brand Archetypes

### The Industry Expert

As an industry expert, you already know everything that there is to know in the field. You probably have enough knowledge and information to give professional advice and guidance to scores of followers and fans. The primary goal of an industry veteran or expert is to spread his knowledge across as many platforms as possible so that the information can reach out to larger groups of individuals.

### The Creator

As the name suggests, the creator is an individual who creates fresh and new content from scratch. This content can be in the form of videos, photos, art, design and several other aspects. The content creator or creator has to handle the entire process from creation to marketing. A creator needs to be able to come up with and share new and creative ideas on a daily basis to create a strong base of followers and fans. For example, Donald Trump can be considered as the perfect example of a creator because of all the towering structures that he has constructed from scratch.

### The Average Joe

In this archetype of personal branding, the individual focuses solely on creating a self-brand. This could mean that he or she shares the adventures of his daily and personal life through blogs and vlogs. Fans and followers of this archetype of personal branding are impressed and intrigued by the individual and their lifestyle that they become a major influencer for them. In this case, the influencer is just a regular person who puts forth his own personal experiences to influence his followers.

## The Curator

The curator compiles lists of the best content or material that is already available in the market and serves this carefully curated list to fans and followers. The curator is not a creator and he doesn't create content from scratch. The curator simply has an eye for existing quality content that can possibly become a trend and makes it aware to their followers. For instance, Kim Kardashian makes the perfect case of the curator because she markets products like cosmetics and clothing that are amongst the best in the industry.

## The Case Study

In this archetype of personal branding, the influencer teaches and influences his followers by first trying and testing things out himself. After they have tested a product or service, they reveal their experiences to his followers in a straightforward and honest way. Most fans and followers trust this form of personal branding because they want an honest and transparent opinion and review on particular products.

### The Journalist

The journalist is a kind of personal brand archetype that is the perfect blend between the creator and the curator. The journalist acts as a new source of information for a specific market. The journalist will make a compilation of trends and events and he or she will also communicate their personal thoughts and reflections.

### The Critic/Instigator

Last but not least is the instigator or critic. This personal brand archetype is best suited for individuals who have an interest in drama. The instigator influences followers and fans by sparking debates, and stir up all kinds of dramatic controversies. The instigator thrives by critiquing others that are related to a specific industry.

Now that you know and understand the 7 archetypes of personal branding, it will become much easier for you to figure out the primary goal of your personal brand. Let's discuss the three main aspects of personal branding so that you can figure out which one of them best suits your style and personality.

# Are You Capable of Becoming an Influencer In Your Own Niche?

The first question that you really need to ask yourself when you're laying down the foundation for your personal brand is whether or not you're capable of becoming an influencer in your own niche. In order for one to be able to influence people from a specific industry or niche, the influencer needs to have a tremendous amount of knowledge and information about the product or industry in general. Followers and fans should be so impressed by the profound knowledge of the influencer that they can directly have an impact on them and influence their thought processes. A person who is capable of being an influencer in their own niche is sort of like the expert of the industry. They should be able to provide proper guidance to his followers and fans. The job of an influencer is to provide accurate information and guide the customer towards purchasing a particular product. Being an influencer is something that can be done only once you have enough people to follow you and are impressed with the information you share.

# Do You Have the Capabilities to Promote Your Own Products?

Not every manufacturer goes out in the market to promote his or her own products. There are some individuals who have the potential and powerful to market and promote their own products, while there are others who don't. You need to find out for yourself whether you have the right tools to influence people to invest in the products that you have to offer. Try to promote your products yourself a few times and if you see a rise in sales and general inquiries for the product, you might just be the influencer your brand needs. If you see no increase in sales or maybe even a drop in sales, maybe you should try to gain some knowledge on how to promote your brand.

## Consider Promoting Products Through Affiliate Marketing

Affiliate marketing is all about passive income by choosing to market and sell products for various brands. For instance, you may choose a product or service you want to market a company and then use social media to create awareness. For every customer or sale that is drawn in through the efforts of the affiliate will result in rewards for you.

When it comes to creating awareness about a product or service for affiliate marketing you need to take into consideration the platform you choose to promote these products and the audience. Try to choose products you're familiar with since this can help you promote it more effectively and you'll be able to provide value-based information to potential customers. When the information you provide is valuable, people notice your presence on social media automatically and you'll manage to increase your followers and generate more sales.

## What Are Your Brand Values?

Creating a personal brand is not just about being able to influence followers and sell products and services. A brand reflects everything that you as an individual stand for. The marketing strategies, company logo, employees, products, and website of a brand may change over time, however, the values of the brand must always remain strong, steady and unchanged. Brand values need to be memorable, actionable, unique, meaningful, timeless, and clear and defined. Some common and popular examples of brand value include integrity, honesty, customer focus, smooth communication, constant improvement, passion for success and so on. You need to take some time to figure out your own personal brand values and adherently stick to them throughout the lifespan of your brand. If you don't have your brand values set in stone, your target market and audience will find it difficult to connect with you. Influencers need to have a certain set of values to attract a crowd that can relate to those values. Influencers who lack stability will only end up failing when it comes to personal branding as no followers will be influenced by an imbalanced brand ambassador.

## Importance of Connection, Authority, And Trust When Promoting Products

As a brand ambassador or a product endorser, you need to make sure that you have an authoritative personality that positively influences your followers and fans. Your positive and inspiring nature should be able to create a connection between you and your followers. Your enterprising personality should allow followers to automatically develop a sense of trust in you. When you build a strong, trustworthy, and authoritative connection with your followers, promoting products to them and influencing them becomes much easier. A seller relies more on maintaining a relationship with the buyer. This can be done through blogs or a company website. On the other hand, an influencer manages to convince the buyer to purchase a product without building too much of a connection. This difference in approach usually brings about a difference in sales numbers.

## Important Factors to Consider to Truly Connect with Your Audience

There are five important factors that you should pay attention to if you want to truly connect with your audience. These include the following:

- Build an actual connection with your audience when you're connecting with them. Tell them real and factual stories of your life. Make them feel like you understand their emotions and thoughts and that you are as much human as any of them. When they see this warm and connective side to you, they will automatically be more interested and intrigued in your personal brand.

- Conduct proper research on your audience and serve them exactly what they are looking for. For instance, if your audience comprises of people who are looking for loyalty and integrity, provide them with these values to build their confidence in you. Research makes a huge difference. You can conduct your own research based on the information you gather on social media, forums, and more.

- Using humor, empathy, and compassion when you're engaging with your audience can prove to be very effective in gaining their loyalty. Your audience wants to know that you understand their problems and plights and can help them through their trials and tribulations.

- Be prepared to answer the questions that the members of your audience may ask you. If you go unprepared and are completely stumped when questioned, it may cost you the interest of your audience members.

Now that you know and understand all the basics of personal branding and brand value, it's time to understand how marketing has evolved from traditional marketing to modern methods of marketing.

# Chapter 2 - Traditional versus Modern Marketing

It is safe to say that over the past few decades the world of marketing has undergone a revolution in terms of marketing methods. While traditional marketing was a one-way street, modern methods of marketing are far more interactive and engaging. Each one of these forms of marketing has its own benefits and drawbacks. While modern marketing focuses more on marketing through social media platforms, traditional marketing tapped into various forms of mass media and communication to send out a message to target markets and prospective customers.

## Different Forms of Traditional Marketing

As it has already been established, traditional marketing methods depended on several different forms of mass media and communication. Here are a few of the forms of traditional marketing that were used to spread a message or market a product or company:

**Television Ads:** Short commercials and advertisements on television shown between programs was one of the most popular methods of advertising. This method was typically used when the audience that needed to be reached out was widespread and large in size. Television-based marketing and advertising are still used quite aggressively.

**Magazine Ads:** Another traditional method of marketing is the placement of advertisements in magazines. Colorful and vibrant ads with a strong message were printed in business, societal, and fashion magazines to capture the attention of readers. This is yet another method of traditional marketing that is still popularly used today.

**Billboards:** Billboards were an immensely popular method of marketing in traditional times, before the introduction of the Internet and social media.

**Newspaper Ads:** Printing advertisements in newspapers was a great way for companies and brands to reach out to the masses a few decades ago.

**Pamphlets, Brochures, Flyers:** Traditional marketing depended a great deal on the distribution of pamphlets, brochures, and flyers. These flyers and pamphlets would be handed out at densely populated locations like city sidewalks and train stations.

**Door-to-Door Marketing:** Marketing executives were sent to different neighborhoods with sample products to market these products from house to house.

**Telemarketing:** Cold calling was another traditional method of marketing that was used to reach out to prospective customers and clients. This traditional method of marketing still proves to be very effective.

**Direct Mail:** Brochures, pamphlets, and sample products were sent out via postal mail to prospective clients back in the day.

These are considered the most effective traditional methods of marketing before the introduction of the Internet. Most companies and brands relied on these old-school marketing methods to create a brand image. A lot of these traditional marketing methods are used even now but with a modern twist. For instance, magazine marketing still prevails but most magazines have now become a part of digital media. Alternatively, pamphlets and brochures are still sent out via mail but through electronic mail. That being said, let's now get into a detailed discussion of modern marketing methods.

# Modern Methods of Marketing

In addition to some of the traditional methods of marketing that are still prevalent, there are numerous modern methods of marketing that have taken the commercial world by storm. Some of these methods include:

**Email:** A large number of business and profit organizations depend on email marketing to deliver a message to customers and clients. Digital brochures, photos, and details of new products and other data are sent over to prospective and existing customers via email.

**Text Message Marketing:** Another highly effective and popular method of modern marketing includes marketing through text messages.

**Social Media:** One can officially say that social media has become one of the most effective methods of marketing. Most organizations and business individuals are restructuring their marketing strategies to market their products and create brand awareness through social media.

## The Interactive Qualities of Social Media Marketing

One thing that makes social media marketing unique compared to other forms of modern marketing is the fact that this method is a highly interactive and engaging one. Most companies usually interact with their customers through their social media pages in the form of replying to comments or even engaging in personal chat.

Platforms like Facebook and Instagram allow you to share a ton of information in the form of posts, videos, photos, and more. This helps to promote the business and opens the door to two-way communication for individuals and the brands. Social media marketing makes it possible for companies and organizations to create a strong relationship with potential clients. There are five main aspects that enable a business organization to create a strong foundation with potential clients, these aspects include the following:

### Community

Social media marketing is all about being able to build a strong community in the digital world. Business organizations create social media pages that are open to the general public and community. These pages contain information about the organization, updates about new products and services, and other pieces of important information. Social media pages are typically followed by existing customers, prospective customers, competitors, and stakeholders of the organization. Business pages on social media platforms make it possible for the various stakeholders of the firm to interact with individuals from the business organization as well as with existing and potential customers.

## *Engagement*

Social media marketing makes it possible to keep stakeholders and potential customers engaged in the events and developments of the business organization. When the organization becomes active on a social media marketing platform, all the latest advancements of the firm are uploaded and shared on the social media group. This enlightens the potential customers on the reliability of the business. Individuals who engage in such businesses are loyal to the brand and tempted to participate in discussion and interaction.

## *Discussions and Interactions*

Social media marketing makes it possible for true interaction between the business organization and other potential and existing customers. For instance, when a business organization creates a social media page and uploads the latest information about a new product, the individuals following the page are able to make comments, share their experiences, and provide their input on the new product. Further, followers of the page are able to interact with one another as well, thereby creating a strong follower list.

## Building a Relationship with the Audience

When individuals from the business organization interact with the audience that follows their social media page, they build a strong relationship with the followers. Most people appreciate it when they are able to get prompt responses to queries on social media marketing pages. When the marketing head responds back swiftly to comments and queries on social media, it increases the trust and confidence that the followers of the page has in the organization. In today's day and age, a majority of individuals end up purchasing products that have good reviews and ratings on social media.

## Showing Concern

Social media marketing makes it possible for a business organization to show genuine concern towards clients and customers. By swiftly responding back to customer grievances and queries, offering detailed information and assistance to prospective clients and so on, clients feel a sense of concern that the business organization has for them. This helps to build stronger and longer lasting business relationships.

These five aspects of social media marketing makes it possible for business organizations to create a strong marketing base for the organization.

## Benefits of Having a Social Media Community

Having a strong social media community is beneficial for several reasons.

- The creation of a social media community makes it possible for a business organization to increase awareness of the business brand. More and more social media users will become acquainted with the brand when posts are shared by the organization and online searches for products and services are conducted by a social media user.

- Social media marketing through community pages helps the business to stay on top of the minds of customers. On average, social media users browse their accounts at least once a day. When new information about the business organization pops up on the news feeds of social media users, the business organization tends to create a form of indirect advertising for prospective and existing customers.

- Another benefit of having a social media community is that it can help to increase website traffic for the business organization. When a post from the website of the business organization is shared on social media, the reader will automatically be tempted to read and learn more and may end up visiting the actual business portal.

- Having a strong social media community is also beneficial because it helps the business organization to find and generate new customer leads. When an individual is browsing through his social media feeds and they stumble upon the community page created by a specific brand or business organization, they may become interested in the products and services offered by the brand. This will encourage the social media user to interact with other individuals from the digital community and it may even end up in a sale.

- Social media communities create a platform where business organizations can directly communicate and interact with customers and clients. The business organizations are able to resolve any issues or queries that clients put forward. Further, in the event of a bad review from a customer, the business organization is able to make public apologies and deal with any crisis in an efficient and swift manner.

- Social media community pages make it possible for business organizations to keep a close watch on competing brands in the industry by following their community pages.

As you can see, having a strong social media community can have a positively profound impact on a business organization and it can also help to build a strong rapport between the brand and its customers. If you're looking to set up your very own social media community, here's what you need to know.

# Tips to Build a Strong Social Media Community

Building a social media community takes a few simple steps.

- The first step towards building a strong social media presence is to understand the needs of your audience. If you're going to end up posting data that is irrelevant to your audience, you may have hundreds of followers but you will be unable to convert those followers into customers. Understand the exact requirements and personas of your followers. Post products and services that you think they will be intrigued to invest in. Understanding your audience will prove to be very effective in developing long-term customer relationships.

- Prospective customers tend to dislike faceless organizations. If you want your social media community page to be a successful one, you need to be interactive and engaging with your customers. Don't be afraid to use a little bit of humor when responding back to customer queries. Have enough humility to apologize when your brand is at fault. Be prompt in responding to complaints.

- Uploading product videos, photos, and using visuals in any way that you can, will definitely be effective in improving your social media standing. Most social media users prefer to watch videos as opposed to reading content.

Now that you know exactly what you need to do to lay down the foundation for a strong social media community, here are a few things you must avoid when building a community.

## Things to Avoid When Building A Social Media Community

When building a social media community you need to avoid the following things:

- Don't get into verbal brawls when engaging and interacting with customers who don't see eye-to-eye with the brand. Gently but firmly try to change their point of view or come to a common ground that's beneficial to both parties.

- Don't take days to respond to customers and clients on the social media community page. You need to be prompt in your responses to avoid losing customers and to build that confidence and faith in your followers.

- Don't anti-campaign when it comes to competitors. Learn to take competition in your stride and strive to be better than your competitors. Negative or snide remarks on competing brands will only end up putting your business in a bad light.

All that being said, another thing that you need to keep in mind when creating a social media community page is that not all your followers are your friends. While your page may have thousands of followers, you must not get carried away. You need to make it a point to be able to distinguish between followers who are genuine prospective clients and ones that are just in for the entertainment. Don't try to please every follower you have on your social media community page as that will only end up backfiring on your business organization or brand. Choose a method of communication that is most relatable to your customers and prospective clients and fiercely stick to that method of communication so that you can build long-term relationships and a strong social media standing.

# Chapter 3 - Target Audience and Message

Now that you have understood the importance and the benefits of having a social media community page, it is important to understand how to reach out to your target audience by sending out the right message. If you want to rope in customers, you need to be able to identify and distinguish them from the crowd. Let's now discuss the various ways in which you can find your audience on social media:

## How to Find Your Audience On Social Media

No matter how fabulous and fantastic your products and services are, they will be of no use if your online content is not being pitched to the correct audience. You can have the most engaging and captivating online content but if you want the content to reach out to prospective customers and clients, you first need to figure out who they are and ensure that your online marketing content is aimed at them.

Here are a few tips on how to find your audience on social media:

# Identifying Your Audience

The first step is identifying the correct audience. You need to figure out things like the age groups that your content reaches out to, the average income of these individuals and groups, and other important data. In addition to understanding the basic psyche and lifestyle of your target audience, you also need to figure out whether the channel that you're using for social media marketing is appropriate for your products and services. For instance, if you're marketing a product that is best suited for individuals between the ages of 35 and 50, then it is advisable to use Facebook as a social media marketing platform. This is because Facebook allows you to market your content to a specific audience by applying filters and by allowing you to select the audience that you wish to attract. Facebook also continues to remain the most used social media platform by a variety of age groups. On the other hand, if you're looking to market a product that is best suited for teenagers and young adults, then Twitter and Instagram marketing are highly recommended as both these platforms are used a lot more by teenagers and a younger audience compared to Facebook. Hence, understanding and identifying the correct audience and the correct social media channel is essential for an impactful marketing campaign.

# Survey Existing Customers

The next step towards finding your audience on social media

is surveying already existing customers. You can ask your customers questions like what the social media platforms they most use are, what kinds of followers they have, whether or not they read blogs on a regular basis, and so on. Once you have conducted a survey, you will have a better idea of how and what platforms to market your content on so that it reaches the correct audience.

## Find Your Target Audience in Facebook Groups

Browsing through Facebook groups can prove to be a very effective way to find new customers and clients. When you browse through groups that are in some way related to the kind of products and services your brand has to offer, there are fair chances that you will be able to rope in a lot of customers from these groups by marketing your content and products to them. However, do keep in mind that in order to be able to gain a customer base from Facebook, you will need to use a personal or individual account and not your community page.

## Tailor Your Content Based on Your Target Audience

Now that you have understood how to identify your target audience, you need to make sure that your content is tailored in a way that it relates to your target audience. Tailoring content is all about putting up engaging posts and creating a well-balanced content plan. You cannot keep posting promotional content every single day or multiple times a day. Excessive promotional content on the news feeds of your target audience will only end up irritating them. Nobody likes to have their feeds overflowing with ads and promotional marketing messages. You should maintain a proper schedule that uploads promotional content only once or twice a week. On the other hand, when it comes to engaging content, you should put up fresh, new engaging posts daily to keep your customers and prospective clients intrigued. Another thing to keep in mind when it comes to marketing content is the fact that most people don't prefer reading text-only posts. The minds of social media users are always captivated when there is visual content along with writing. When you're putting up a promotional or engaging post on your social media community page, you need to make sure that you also include a few photos or videos so that the minds of your target audiences are captured.

# Put Up Personal and Real Content

Content marketing is not just about putting up posts about products and services. Most target audiences are interested in dealing with actual people and not just faceless organizations. It is important that you put up posts that include the actual faces behind the organization, their trust in the organization will tend to build.

Finding your target audience on social media is simple as long as you follow the aforesaid steps carefully. Once you have understood the psyche of your target audience, it will become much easier for you to create content that your audience will be able to relate to. Appropriate content on your community page will attract more and more social media browsers and you will end up increasing the numbers of followers that you have on your page.

## Sending Out a Message to Followers And Target Audiences

Identifying your target audience is only one half of the game, the next step is sending out the correct message to your target audience. When it comes to sending the perfect message, there are several things to take into consideration. Here's what you need to know:

## Create Content That Is in Sync With Your Brand Values

When you're creating content for the brand's community page, you need to make sure that the content is in sync with the values that your brand stands for. For instance, if your brand believes in honesty, integrity, and customer satisfaction, then the content that you upload on the community page should be able to reflect these values to followers, clients, and prospective customers. If you upload content that is contrary to your brand values, you will only end up sending mixed signals to readers and viewers. When followers get mixed signals from social media content, they tend to lose their faith and trust in the brand and the business organization. So, when putting together content for your social media community, always make sure that it is on par with your brand values.

## Ensure Your Personal Branding Strategy is Appropriate

If you're going for the personal branding marketing strategy, you need to make sure that your brand ambassador is someone who your target audience can relate to. For instance, if you're marketing real estate inventory and you choose to use Kim Kardashian as your brand ambassador, your target audience will never be able to relate to the fashionista. If you're marketing cosmetics and makeup products and you choose to partner with a tech genius as your brand ambassador, your target audience will not see the correlation. Hence, it is very important that the brand ambassador you choose should be relatable to your target audience. Find a brand ambassador that your target audience will be interested in following.

Let's now understand what it is about a celebrity or a brand ambassador that makes other people follow them:

## *Why Do People Follow Other People?*

In most cases, people follow celebrities, brand ambassadors, and successful individuals because they aspire to be like them. They are motivated by enterprising brand ambassadors and want to improve their own lives to become successful by following the example of these celebrities. People follow famous personalities with the intention of learning from them. They make celebrities their role models. In some cases, people also follow celebrities purely for entertainment purposes. They want to know what is going on in the personal lives of the rich and famous. They also want to follow what they wear, eat, and even where they go. All in all, people follow other people for a variety of reasons that include motivation, inspiration, and entertainment. So when you're choosing a brand ambassador for personal branding, make sure that you choose wisely.

# How to Send a Message to Your Target Audience

Sending a message to your target audience can be tricky business. If you don't draft the message in a way that's relatable to your audience, it will end in disaster. Here are a few tips that you can follow while drafting the message:

- Make sure that the content that you put down addresses the main concerns of your target audience. In order to be able to do this, you need to know and understand the thinking and psyche of your target audience very well. There are various ways you can research your potential customer, and social media groups is one of them.

- Secondly, the tone that your message carries plays a very important role in impacting your audience. You need to ensure that the message is always respectful to the audience. You can make the message more light-hearted by using a bit of humor too.

- Using visuals when sending out a message to your audience can also prove to be extremely effective. People tend to get bored reading copious amounts of written text and they can sometimes lose interest in reading the content midway. You can post videos, photos, and other visual content to keep the reader captivated and interested in your message.

- Being informative in your message can also be very impactful in capturing the attention of your target audience. Share information that your audience is probably unaware of and would love to learn about. Provide them with new data that will help them to use your products and services in a way that is beneficial to them.

## Things to Avoid When Sending a Message to Your Target Audience

Now that you know what you need to do in order to capture the attention of your target audience when you're sending out a message to them, you should also keep in mind that there are certain things that you absolutely must avoid when drafting a message:

- Don't deviate off topic and provide information that is absolutely irrelevant to your target audience. This will only cause frustration and disinterest in the audience and they may eventually switch to competing brands.

- Don't send out multiple messages back-to-back when dealing with your target audience. Too much information can cause confusion and irritability among your audience. Maintain a fixed amount of time between messages so that the information that you're sharing can sink in with the audience.

- Avoid bad mouthing your competitors at all costs. Bad mouthing your competitors will more so speak badly of you than of them.

All in all, reaching out to your target audience and sending out the right message is easy. All you need to do is to identify your target audience and give them exactly what they are looking for by providing relatable content and using brand ambassadors. The next step towards marketing your personal brand is having the correct sales funnel.

# Chapter 4 – How To Monetize Your Personal Brand

Alongside marketing, most business organizations follow the sales funnel process to sell goods and services to customers and prospective clients. The sales funnel process comprises of a few main steps. These steps can be used in synchronization with social media marketing to gain customers.

## Awareness Phase

The awareness phase is the first step of the sales funnel. In this phase, the prospective customer is made aware of the existence of the product or service. In a store or boutique, the client will be made aware of the product by browsing through the available products. In the case of media marketing, you can make your target audience aware of the product by doing a write up of the product on your community page and also by sharing some images and videos of the product.

## Interest Phase

The next phase of the sale funnel is the interest phase. In this phase, the prospective client shows an interest in the products or the services that your brand has to offer. In the case of media marketing, the interest in the prospective client can be piqued by showcasing the features and functioning of the products on your community page.

## Evaluation Phase

The evaluation phase of the sales funnel is a process where the prospective client or customer begins to evaluate and compare competitor's products with your products. They will compare the features of the products of all brands and see which product is the most financially viable and most efficient and useful. When it comes to media marketing, you will have to offer more than your competitors. Prompt responses to queries, engaging and captivating content.

## Decision Phase

In the decision phase of the sales funnel, the prospective client makes a final decision on which product or service to purchase. When a buyer is in the decision phase, he or she will want the best solution. They will be very decisive with regards to the vendor that they may want to purchase from. The buyers evaluate all pros and cons in this phase and then decide on the vendor. The decision phase helps buyers make the right decision.

# Purchase Phase

In the purchase phase of the sales funnel, a final purchase is made by the customer and the payment is handed over to the brand or business organization. In social media marketing, you can share the link to your online shopping portal where the customer can make a purchase for the product or service.

# Personal Branding and the Sales Funnel

Now that you know and understand the basic concept of a sales funnel, let's discuss how you can intertwine your personal branding with the sales funnel. When you're selecting a brand ambassador for your company or brand, you need to make sure that the ambassador is someone who your prospective clients can relate to. When Kim Kardashian markets a cosmetic product, her fans and followers will automatically be tempted to buy it. However, if Donald Trump was to market the same cosmetic product, it would not result in the same effect. In addition to choosing the right brand ambassador, another very important point to keep in mind is selecting one that can pitch the product in a convincing way. Most buyers are tempted to purchase products when they can relate to the behavior and lifestyle of the brand ambassador. If the brand ambassador is someone who they look up to or wish to be like, they will be more interested in investing in or purchasing the products that the ambassador promotes. Personal branding has a great influence on buyer purchase behavior.

## What Influences Buyer Purchase Behavior?

Besides an obvious need for a specific product, buyers are often tempted to purchase products purely on an emotional basis. When a brand ambassador of a specific product has the power to influence a certain target audience, the audience automatically becomes tempted to purchase the product that is being promoted. Influencers have a strong presence that their followers often want to emulate. When they see their influencers promoting cosmetics or specific services, they too wish to be owners and receivers of such products and services respectively. Being able to emotionally seduce a prospective customer into making a product purchase is one of the most popular marketing methods. A large number of brands and firms resort to this method to make large-scale sales.

In addition to emotionally-driven purchases, there are a few other factors that also have an impact on the buyer's purchase behavior. These factors include the following:

## Purchasing Power

Irrespective of how strongly influenced a prospective buyer is by the brand ambassador, the buyer needs to have purchasing power in order to be able to buy a product or service. It is very important that the brand ambassador influences the type of target market that actually has purchasing power. If you're going to market a product worth thousands, when your target audience has a budget in the hundreds range, your entire marketing strategy will prove to be useless. Hence, it is very important that you segment your customers based on their buying capacity for excellent results.

## Group Influence

The immediate social group of a prospective buyer also tends to influence his or her purchase decisions. Family members, friends, relatives, work colleagues, and classmates can directly impact the decision of purchase of the buyer. When the majority of the social circle ends up using a particular product or service, the purchase decision of the buyer in question also tends to tip towards the common preference of his social circle. When it comes to social media marketing and personal branding, you need to make sure that the marketing strategy affects and influences large social groups and not just individuals.

## Marketing and Advertising Campaigns

The marketing and advertising campaign of a brand or business organization has a direct impact on the buying behavior of a purchaser. When a business organization runs an ad or marketing campaign at regular intervals, the organization or brand has a greater chance of influencing prospective buyers to purchase the products that are being promoted. With social media marketing, it has become a lot easier and a lot less costly for business organizations to promote their goods and services. Having an excellent social media marketing strategy can play a profound role in influencing your target audience to make a purchase.

## Personal Preferences

The personal preferences of a buyer also have an impact on their purchasing behavior. There are several purchasers who show brand loyalty towards a brand that they have been using for several years. Converting brand loyal customers can be an uphill task. The only way a social media marketing campaign can attempt to convert a brand loyal customer and convince them to switch brands is by offering more than the brand they are accustomed too.

## A Need for Validation

Most people who go out shopping usually take a friend or family member along with them. This is because the buyer needs some sort of validation that makes him feel that he/she is making the correct purchase decision. Buyers are always doubtful and uncertain about whether their purchase decision is a correct one. Hence, when creating a social media marketing strategy, the brand ambassador or personal branding should provide the validation that the buyer is looking for.

## Decision Anxiety/Customer Objections

Some purchasers tend to suffer from decision anxiety. They are unable to decide between multiple products and they cannot make a final decision on which product to purchase. In such situations, if too much information about the features of the various products is presented to the buyer, they will become even more anxious and disarrayed. The best media marketing strategy in such instances is providing the target audience with a limited and filtered selection. A filtered selection will reduce the purchaser's confusion and anxiety and will enable them to make a quick decision on the product that is best suited for them.

## The "Special" Customer

There are some customers who need to be made to feel special so that they can be influenced to make a final purchase. These customers want the exceptional shopping experience and want sales staff and marketing teams to go to all ends of the earth to provide that special feeling. In your media marketing strategy, you can make these customers feel special by sending them pre-sale email invites, offering them newly launched products before they are marketed on social media and other platforms, and by providing them with limited edition products and exclusive memberships.

## The "Me First" Customer

"Me first" customers are only interested in being the first to get their hands on a brand-new product. Such customers are very brand conscious and tend to enjoy showing off. The best social media marketing strategy for such consumers is one that is based on an extravagant and luxurious lifestyle as opposed to one that's based on the technical aspects and features of the product in question.

## The Shopaholic

It doesn't take much convincing to get a shopaholic to make a purchase. They shop because retail therapy makes them happy. These are the real emotional shoppers. They shop when they are happy, they shop when they are sad, they shop just because. The social media marketing strategy in such cases should be all about providing information on new and never-before-seen products to shoppers.

As you can see, there are several emotional factors that affect the buying behavior of an individual. When you're creating a social media marketing strategy, you need to make sure that you consider these emotional factors and draw up a marketing plan that will influence your target audience. Triggering the emotions of your target audience plays a very important role in social media marketing. This is because when target audiences are moved or pushed on an emotional level that they can relate to, it becomes easier to convert them into long-term buyers and loyal customers. Frame your marketing strategy based on the emotional behavioral patterns of your target audience for good sales.

Now that you know all about personal branding, social media marketing, consumer behaviors, and target audiences, let's discuss the four main channels of social media marketing. Most business organizations and brands are dependent on Facebook, LinkedIn, Instagram and YouTube for their social media marketing. Each one of these four social media platforms has its own benefits and advantages. Facebook as a social media platform is best suited for companies and brands that are trying to create a strong digital community. Facebook is still one of the most used social media platforms and it attracts members of all age groups. Instagram as a social media platform best suited for companies that wish to promote their products and services through visual content (photos and videos). LinkedIn is best suited when a brand or business organization wishes to connect with individuals from the same industry as it acts as the best digital professional networking platform out there. Lastly, YouTube can be used for countless marketing purposes. From uploading ads and promotional videos on new products and services to sharing informational videos about industrial developments and more, YouTube can prove to be a very creative and effective social media marketing platform. Let's now get into a detailed discussion on how to build your personal brand on social media.

# Section 2: Building your Personal Brand

## Chapter 5 - Overview of Different Channels

Building a personal brand on a social media platform requires a lot of planning. You can't just wake up one morning, create a social media account and hope and pray that customers flock to buy the goods and services that your brand has to offer. You need to have a proper marketing strategy and you need a brand ambassador that will rope in the customers. You also need to keep in mind that different channels of social media require different strategies of marketing as each channel may have a different target audience from the other. Let's now discuss the 4 main channels of social media marketing and how you can build your brand on each one of these channels.

## Facebook

Facebook is without a doubt one of the most used social media platforms. This platform has members of all age groups, genders, ethnicities, backgrounds, and races. Most Facebook users end up using their Facebook account at least once a day.

Considering how popular smartphones have gotten, most social media interactions these days are via mobile. This social media platform is one of the most popularly used platforms for marketing and advertising. Since Facebook is such a widely used platform, you can find a wide and never-ending range of target markets and audiences on the platform.

Building your personal brand on Facebook can be a little tricky because you will end up having a great number of followers but not all your followers will be in your target market. When creating a personal brand on Facebook, you need to make sure that your marketing strategy is relevant only to your target audience. There are several ways in which marketing and brand promotion can be done on Facebook. Let's discuss a few of these marketing ideas:

- Create Your Own Community Page - Creating your very own community page on Facebook can prove to be an excellent marketing strategy. Brand awareness and product promotions become a lot easier with a community page on Facebook. It is very important for a brand or business organization to show its human side on a Facebook community page. Interacting with clients and customers, keeping clients engaged with informative articles about products and the industry in general, sharing links to interesting videos, and communicating with your followers is very important.

- Facebook Ads - Classic Facebook ads that pop up on the news feeds of Facebook users is another excellent and effective way to increase and build the image of your personal brand and company name among target audiences. These ads usually comprise of an image of the product, a link to the company website or shopping portal, a few basic details of the products and other types of data. Facebook ads are very useful if you are looking to reach out to specific audiences. The features of these ads include demographic targeting, ad budget setting options, ad testing and more.

- Hosting Facebook Contests - By hosting Facebook contests and getting participants to comment, you can increase the awareness of your business organization or brand to a great extent. Alternatively, you can also use a third-party app to create a contest and add a link to your Facebook community page so that target audiences are able to participate. These interactive contests are fun for target audiences and at the same time will give you a basic idea of the needs, preferences, and likes of your prospective clients and customers.

- Promoted Facebook Posts - Facebook offers the option of promoted posts at a fixed flat rate. Promoted posts come in handy when you want your post to pop up on the news feeds of your target audience. In most cases, the news feeds of Facebook users are overflowing with information and data and often a non-paid promotional post that you upload won't show up on the news feeds of the audience. With the promoted posts marketing option, the post will show up not only on the feeds of your existing followers but they will also pop up on the feeds of your followers' friends.

- Sponsored Stories - Sponsored stories are another great way to spread brand awareness to your target audience. You can put up interesting product photos, short bits of information and other details in your stories. Stories are like video ads of a few seconds that should be engaging enough to capture the attention of the viewer.

# Instagram

When it comes to marketing on Instagram, the entire game changes. Instagram may be owned by Facebook, but its platform is entirely different. Instagram is better suited for visual content as opposed to written content. Unlike Facebook, Instagram is more often used by younger generations than people of all ages. It is an excellent platform to market luxury brands, fashion brands, and lifestyles brands. You can put up videos of your products, stories for upcoming products and other content. Let's now discuss the various aspects of Instagram marketing:

- A Business Profile is a Must - Switching to a business profile on Instagram can prove to be of great help. With a business profile, your target audiences and customers can directly contact you by clicking on the contact button. Further, you can create your very own ads without needing to be dependent on Facebook advertising tools. Also, with an Instagram business profile, your promotional posts are more likely to pop up on the feeds of your followers, making them aware of the latest products and services that your business organization or brand has to offer.

- Collaborate with Influencers - Connecting with the

right influencers on Instagram can also play a very important role in increasing the awareness of your brand name on this social media platform. When there are influencers who have already done the groundwork of building a long list of followers, getting the influencers to market your product or page through mentions and hashtags can increase your followers too. If powerful influencers are promoting your brand, their followers and fans will most likely be tempted to invest in the products that your brand has to offer. Influencers do cost money though, so if you're planning on roping one in you may have to shell out quite a bit of money

- Be Smart With Hashtags - Using the right hashtags when you upload a post on Instagram is crucial. Tons of Instagram users follow specific hashtags. If you want to attract prospective clients and customers, you need to use hashtags that they can relate to and hashtags that are related to your product. For instance, if you have a jewelry brand, you can use a hashtag that is something like #jewelry. The correct hashtags will rope in more and more prospective customers and buyers.

- Have an Excellent and Up-to-Date Bio - Creating a powerful business bio with an eye-catching profile picture, an engaging and intriguing bio, a proper website link, and an account name that is easy to search is very important in getting more followers on your Instagram business profile.

- Boost Your Posts - Boosting posts for a basic cost can also prove to be very effective in increasing brand awareness. The boosted posts end up reaching widespread audiences that aren't already following your page. You can personally select the demographics of the audience that you wish to reach out to or use the auto select option where your posts will reach out to audiences that are similar to your existing followers.

- Have a Proper Marketing Strategy - Lastly, having a proper content marketing strategy is very important when it comes to Instagram promotions. You need to make sure that the content that you share is relevant and relatable to your followers. Further, you need to upload new posts on a timely and consistent basis to keep your followers engaged and to retain your followers. Consistency in posting plays a very important role if you wish to see positive results in sales.

# YouTube

YouTube is a social media channel that has become a hit among people of all ages and people from around the globe. Homemakers are finding themselves glued to YouTube to find new and improved cooking recipes, young people have turned to YouTube for all the latest film trailers and music videos, artists and creators are constantly scouring YouTube for ideas and inspiration. Marketing your brand on YouTube is an excellent way to reach out to larger target markets and audiences. Let's discuss how to increase your company's brand image through YouTube marketing:

- Create Your Own YouTube Channel - Creating a YouTube channel is the first step you need to take to start marketing on YouTube. Your YouTube channel should be designed in a way that's relevant to your brand values.

- Use Interesting Titles - It is very important that you use interesting titles when you upload a video on your YouTube channel. Using the right keywords, keeping the title short, and creating relevant titles can play a vital role in helping you to reach out to your target audience. When creating a catchy title, try giving away maximum information. You should also try to generate curiosity by leaving out certain information out. If you're promoting a weight loss supplement you should try using titles that grab attention and coax people to read the entire article to get all the information. For example, *"It's Time To Get Slim Without The Gym"*. While this gives away little information, it holds on to the core idea but generates curiosity at the same time.

- Upload Clear Videos - When uploading videos on YouTube, you need to make sure that the clarity of the video that you upload is immaculate. HD quality videos are best suited for a good YouTube channel. Target audiences lose interest in watching videos if they aren't of good quality.

- Keep Videos Under a Time Limit - When uploading videos, make sure that you keep videos short and sweet. Videos under five-minutes are most watched on YouTube. Your target audience may not have the time or patience to sit through videos that run for a half hour or longer. Keep the videos short but informative and at the same time make sure that they are engaging.

- Bring in a Brand Ambassador into a YouTube Video - If your company has an influential and powerful brand ambassador, getting the brand ambassador to appear on your YouTube channel can prove to be a very effective form of marketing. Your followers who are influenced and motivated by the brand ambassador will most definitely want to watch the video you upload of your brand ambassador giving a talk or speech.

- Share Your Videos on Other Platforms - Sharing the links of the videos that you upload on YouTube onto other social media platforms can also be very effective in increasing brand awareness and promoting your company and its various products and services.

## LinkedIn

Last but not least is the LinkedIn social media platform. This platform is an excellent network to connect with other professionals. Employers and business organizations can find job seekers, contacts from the industry, and other professionals on this platform. While you may not be able to market goods and services on LinkedIn as you would on Facebook or Instagram, you can still build a pretty strong network on this social media platform. You can grow your email marketing list with the help of LinkedIn. You can also join and create groups that are related to your industry on this platform. Lastly, creating your very own company or brand page on LinkedIn is a great way to create awareness of the business and attract target audiences and professionals from the industry.

So as you can see, there are 4 main channels of social media that are ideal to help you market your personal brand and grow your business. These channels are the most resorted to methods of social media marketing as they are inexpensive, effective, and can reach out to a wide target audience. In comparison to a television ad or a newspaper ad, a social media ad will probably cost you half the amount and it will reach out to ten times as large an audience. The introduction of social media changed the dynamics of the marketing world. Most businesses went digital to promote their brands on a global scale as opposed to promoting them only on a local level. You too can build your brand image and create awareness amongst target audiences by resorting to social media marketing.

It is important for businesses to be on social media, but choosing which social media platform you need to pay most attention to is vital because this decision determines the success or failure of the social media marketing techniques you implement.

Although most business owners believe it's important for them to establish business pages on all social media platforms and stay as active as possible on all these platforms, this should not always be the case. Every business is different and there is a particular social media platform that is right for your business. In order for you to figure out which social media platform works best for your brand, you need to dig a little deeper.

# Understand Your Customer

In order for you to talk to the right customers, you need to first understand their behavior. Depending on the nature of your business you will determine which segment you are targeting in order to look for the right customers. While Facebook is a large platform where you may find people from almost all age groups, social media platforms like Instagram and Twitter are more refined. If your brand appeals to the younger generation, then Instagram is definitely the place for you to be. If you are looking for more prominent and high profile or high-end customers, there is a higher chance you will find them on Twitter.

You also need to understand what your customers look for on these platforms. If you are in the retail sector, establishing strong social media pages on Pinterest and Instagram, where virtual marketing plays a huge role, will benefit you more than platforms like Twitter. If you are in a service-based industry then Facebook and Twitter turn out to be more effective as text-based advertisements are what these customers tend to look for.

# Understanding Each Social Media Platform

If you want to talk with the right kind of customers you need to understand these platforms so you can choose the right one to market your business on.

## Twitter

Twitter is a social media network that allows posts with a word limit. It is for business owners and high-end individuals who tend to look for fast-paced and ever-changing ideas. The information on Twitter needs to be precise, to the point, and fresh.

## Facebook

Facebook is a great place to find customers as it's probably one of the widest networks today. People on Facebook range between the ages of 18 to 60. So, finding a customer here is not going to be a problem. Businesses that cater to people from various age groups will definitely benefit from Facebook the most. You can choose different kinds of advertisement plans on Facebook and you can also switch between images videos or text depending on what you think will work best for you.

## Pinterest

If you want to share your ideas in through visual creation then Pinterest is one of the best platforms to pick. You can also target specific users on interest who look for certain products on the site.

## Instagram

There is a huge hype around Instagram when it comes to the

younger generation today. Like Pinterest, Instagram is also a visual site and if you know your product is visually appealing and can attract attention, Instagram is the best site for you.

*YouTube*

If images and texts don't do the job, videos surely will. There are a ton of business ideas out there that need to be demonstrated to the public and that's where YouTube comes into the picture. If you are selling an appliance or a gadget, people want to know how it works and what the functions are. In this scenario, YouTube is your best bet.

## Social Media to Build Your Personal Brand

Businesses are still struggling to figure out how to create maximum online branding with the least investment. Different business owners have different approaches but if you are looking for the best techniques that will work on any social media platform you need to begin by picking one social media platform you know will suit your business best. Once you narrow down your selection you can then plan your strategies ahead.

## Find the Right Groups

Social media platforms like Facebook and LinkedIn have various groups that focus on a certain industry or specific topic. If you want to create brand awareness around your product, you need to target these groups and start your promotion from there. While the competition in these groups is high, there is a strong chance you will grab the attention of people who are interested in your services and they will get in touch with you.

## Keep Your Image Consistent

While you should target one social media platform if spending money on social media marketing, it's important for you to have social media pages across all platforms. When you establish social media pages on various platforms, you need to stay consistent with the image you use. This image helps to build a brand and people can relate to this image when they think of your business. Constantly changing the images on various social media platforms will confuse people and they won't be able to relate to your business as well. Consistency is essential when it comes to establishing a brand so do not compromise on image/logo quality and take your time to pick one that you are going to stick to long term.

## Engage Regularly

Irrespective of what social media platform you choose, regular interaction is essential. If you do not post on a regular basis, people will forget about your brand. You need to constantly remind them about your business, the services you provide or the products you sell as well, as various offers from time to time. While it is important for you to engage regularly with the audience, you need to remember that over-posting isn't good either. If you post too many times in a day, people will get frustrated and tend to unfollow you.

## Diversify Your Content

Sharing the same format on a regular basis could get boring to the audience. If you want people to stay interested in your business, you need to think out of the box and come up with unique and interesting ways to share content on various platforms. If you are promoting your business on platforms like LinkedIn or Facebook, you can choose to spruce up your marketing strategies by incorporating a video every now and then or sharing a funny meme. If you do something different and people like it, the chances that they will share your content also increases.

## Study Influencers

Influencers have a huge fan following and this tells us that they doing something right. If you want to get the kind of exposure an influencer has, you need to think like them. Look at what they do on a regular basis and try to develop a plan based on that. When you are choosing an influencer, try to pick one who relates to your business because that will help you understand what you need to do for your business. You can find them on relevant social media pages and Instagram too!

## Ask Questions

Social media marketing does not have to be a one-way interaction with the audience. The best way to get in touch with potential customers is to ask them questions. It increases the chances of conversation and it also lets you know what your customers or potential customers think about your business.

## Jump into Discussions

Participating in discussion on social media platforms is a smart thing to do. It shows people you are responsive and you engage in various activities on the platform. People who have shied away from commenting on posts you've shared will consider doing it because they believe you will respond to them. When you choose to participate in a discussion, make sure you have a positive impact on a discussion. People tend to move away from businesses that speak ill about a competitor in discussions. If you want to share information, make sure you share positive information about your business without putting others down.

## Monitor Your Name

There are tons of social media platforms out there and it is beneficial for your business to try and figure out which platform works well through a little experimentation. Once you've tried out various social media platforms, you can then monitor your name to see how your business is trending on each platform.

# Chapter 6 - Facebook Marketing and Advertising

Ever since Mark Zuckerberg introduced Facebook to the world, things haven't been the same. Love it or hate it, you can't ignore the presence of Facebook in our lives. With a social media platform as big and popular as Facebook, it's only a matter of time before you realize how important the social media platform is to your business.

If you're looking to establish a brand online, starting with Facebook isn't a bad idea. Facebook has one of the largest user bases across the globe which means it will have a strong impact on your business.

Creating a strong impact is one thing but making sure it's positive is another. If you want to self-promote your business on Facebook, you need to take your time and make sure you do it the correct way. You have to remember that a lot of competition is out there. One small mistake could go viral and escalate, thereby hampering the integrity and brand name of your business permanently. If you want to make it big on Facebook, make sure you get your research done correctly so you can create a brand that everyone loves.

Facebook is the perfect place for you to brand your business because the platform is diverse and there are plenty of marketing tools on the platform. Unlike Instagram or YouTube, where you can only share pictures or videos, Facebook gives you the freedom to do it all. This also allows you to experiment with various marketing techniques to see what suits your business best. If you want to establish a brand on Facebook, you should follow the right strategies to help make your brand a strong and positive one.

## Define Your Business

When you start out on Facebook the first thing you need to do is let people know what your business is all about. The information does not need to be overly lengthy. When entering information on your Facebook page, you need to make sure the information you enter here is consistent with the information you have entered on other social media platforms. This makes it easier and more convenient for your potential customers to relate to the brand and identify and follow you on multiple platforms. The important thing you need to remember when defining a brand is choosing something that is self-explanatory. This means that the picture you choose as the brand image needs to tell people about your business and what it is, rather than them having to figure it out on their own.

## Learn Who Your Followers and Fans Are

It's important for you to know the kind of people who come to your social media page. This gives you a clear idea of the kind of people you are attracting to your business and whether or not it fits your criteria. Spending money on social media advertisements can be effective, but if you end up attracting people who do not benefit from your business in any way then that promotion is of no good.

## Choose a Good Strategy

This is perhaps one of the most important things that you need to keep in mind when marketing your brand on Facebook. You have to decide on a strategy that ensures you don't overspend but still benefit out of it. Social media marketing is very lucrative and some businesses end up spending a huge amount of their marketing budget, believing that they can get good results. While social media marketing is great, it's important you know how to do it right before you invest too much money. The best way to get a strong strategy in place is to research other brands and see what helped them become a name in the market.

## Turn Off Tagging

You may want people to interact with you and constantly share information on your page, but tagging isn't the best thing to do. While it may be good for others, you should know that it has repercussions as well. If somebody somewhere does not like your brand or hasn't benefited from it as much as they would like to, they might lash out. When you are starting out and establishing a brand, the last thing you want is negative promotion on your page. It is better to glance through all the information shared before it goes live on the page.

## Create a Vanity URL

In case you didn't already know this, a vanity URL is a URL that consists of your business name at the end of the hyperlink. For example, if your business name is Viral Squads, the best vanity URL to choose would be - www.facebook.com/viralsquads. This makes your brand more accessible and people tend to recognize it a lot faster.

## Post Updates

Post updates are something that is standard on all social media platforms. You need to make sure you have somebody to do this regularly if you want to establish a brand online. When it comes to posting updates on social media platforms, you need to understand that each platform has different regulations, or unspoken rules, as we call it. Although there are no hard-set rules that you can't post 'x' number of times on a platform, it's always better to do your research and post according to what works best depending on which platform you are posting on. In regard to Facebook, it makes more sense to post early in the morning, one post around noon, and then one at the end of the day. You can also use analytic tools to your advantage. These tools will tell you when your potential customers are active and it will help you to garner more attention to your page.

## Link Your Facebook Page to Other Social Media Pages

Linking your page is important because it helps you increase your followers on all these pages. The stronger your presence on multiple social media platforms, the better the chances of your brand becoming something bigger. You don't have to spend marketing funds on all these platforms; you just need to think in a smart way.

## Use Events to Your Advantage

Facebook has an interesting page called 'Events'. Once you have a certain number of followers on your fan page, you can start creating events to let people know of a launch of a new product or even an upcoming sale. When you treat your customers exclusively, they feel special and they will keep coming back to you brand, which helps you to establish brand loyalty.

Facebook has a lot of users - this increases the chances of you getting more potential customers via this social media platform. If you want to target the right customers on

Facebook, it's important to plan every move. While there are over a billion users on Facebook, not all these users are not your potential customers. You need to narrow down your selection and target people who will benefit your business as opposed to creating awareness among people who are not going to benefit from your business.

Facebook is a smart social media platform that allows you to narrow down your advertisements on various demographics. Some of these include location, ethnicity, language, behavior, age group, and even interests.

## Components of a Facebook Advertisement

While most social media platforms allow you to have only certain kinds of advertisements that you can use, Facebook allows you to experiment. There are different kinds of advertisements you can place on Facebook depending on what you think will work best for your target audience.

### Text Advertisements

A text advertisement is a short advertisement that lets people know about the kind of services you provide. These advertisements works best for service-based businesses that don't have a product to sell. If you want your text advertisements to work out well, you need to make sure the text is catchy and interesting.

## Image-Based Advertisements

Image-based advertisements are best for businesses that are selling products. In order for you to promote a product, it is always better to place an image of the actual product and have a little text with the image along with a link to purchase the product.

## Description

Facebook allows you to place an advertisement of about 250 characters. You need to get as creative as possible with this description so you can let people know about all the information they are looking for, prior to purchasing the product. You also need to include the link of the product in this description itself.

## Caption

The caption or the heading of the advertisement needs to be interesting in order for people to want to read on. Don't have a lengthy caption, but, at the same time, you need to make sure that it's not too short either. It's best to have a creative team come up with interesting captions that grab the attention of users.

## Call-to-Action

While you should provide a link with every advertisement, you also need to tell potential customers what to do. A 'call-to-action' like 'subscribe to this page' or 'click here for more' is something that you should include in any advertisement irrespective of what kind of advertisement you are using.

## The Importance of the Right Design

When you place an advertisement on Facebook, you need to pay a lot of attention to its design. The more emphasis you put on design, the better the response. An attractive image always works better in comparison to a 'text only' advertisement. This will help you to get the attention of your potential customers. Colors are also important - you need to make sure that the colors will make the advertisement stand out among the rest.

## Targeting the Right Audience

Since Facebook gives you the opportunity of targeting an audience based on various preferences, it's easy to cut down your list and figure out which of these people are your best potential customers. Even with the filters in demographics, it is always better to narrow down your search even further by combining two or three demographics together so you get the best possible outcome.

# Goal of Facebook Marketing

Social media marketing benefits your business in various ways. Facebook is one of the most popular platforms to choose from. When you choose Facebook advertisement, it's important for you to understand what you are going to gain out of the activity. This is important because you will be able to approach Facebook marketing with the right expectations.

# Building a Brand in The Community

If you are a local business owner, the most important thing is to create awareness among people in the community. When you start Facebook marketing, you need to narrow down your filters to create maximum impact around these areas so you get visibility where it matters most.

# Customer Service

Apart from being able to promote your business on Facebook, you also need to be able to promote effective customer service to potential and existing. Just because someone is already a customer does not mean you should ignore them. Facebook marketing isn't only about getting new customers but also about maintaining good relationships with existing ones if you expect brand loyalty and repeat customers.

# Fan Page

Your fan page is a page which your customers will follow. Anything posted on the fan page will be visible to your customers so it is important for you to keep them informed. Apart from spending money on social media marketing by using Facebook as a channel, you also need to regularly share content on your fan page so your existing followers know what your business is up to and they can stay informed on upcoming sales or offers.

# Social Media Mistakes to Avoid on Facebook

Marketing on Facebook has gained a lot of popularity. Almost all business owners are trying to market products on this platform because of its demand and the number of users on the site. Marketing your business on Facebook is great, but doing it without knowing what exactly needs to be done, could create problems for your business. A social media reputation is something that can either improve or destroy a business. In order for your business to grow and establish a strong brand name in a positive manner, you need to avoid the major mistakes that some business owners end up making in the course of marketing their business.

You need to understand that social media is an exposed platform and everything you say or do on it is visible by almost everyone which is why you need to take your decisions seriously. There are a lot of things you should do, however, here are a list of things that you certainly should not do.

## *Not Creating a Social Media Strategy*

Just because social media marketing is a trend doesn't mean you have to jump into it instantaneously. The best way to get into social media is to explore and understand how it's going to benefit your business. Facebook is a great place to promote your business but you also need to understand what strategies you need to apply in order to market your business better. The smartest way to do this would be to go through your competitors' Facebook pages and see what they are doing. Put yourself in the shoes of a customer and imagine what you would have liked to see on that page and what you didn't like. Do this for a couple of businesses and take notes before you create your own strategy. The benefit of doing this is that you will manage to get a clear concept and strategy that will be more effective than the already existing one.

Apart from looking at what your competitors do, you also need to take into consideration your own requirements which include: the audience you plan on targeting, the amount of money and time that you are ready to invest, and the end goal. The goal for every business is different and while some businesses just want to create awareness about the business online, there are others who are looking to sell. If you want to sell your products on Facebook, you need to be more involved in the process because this ensures you are taking responsibility for the kind of products you sell.

### Not Selecting a Target Audience

Once you have decided what you want to do on Facebook in terms of marketing, you then need to decide how you're going to segregate the audience. If you have a global presence and your business is accessible all over the world, it's easier for you to market on Facebook. But if you have a limited geographic area you are targeting, you may need to filter down the audience based on your preferences. A key aspect about Facebook is that there are multiple filters you can use and these filters come in handy when you want to sort out the kinds of people you are looking for. You can also filter these people by checking out those who are interested in your services. While this leaves you with a very small number of people, these are usually the kind of people who would be the first customers.

### Dealing with Negative Feedback

When you plan on marketing on social media, you need to be prepared for negative feedback and backlash from customers from time to time. No matter how good you think your brand is, there are going to be hiccups in certain areas which may not be in your control and you need to be prepared for this.

One of the major mistakes business owners make when promoting on social media is ignoring negative comments or replying to them with equally negative remarks. When you are on social media, the one thing you need to keep in mind is that there are going to be a lot of eyes on you and the way you react to negative situations can create a huge impact on your business. If you want to keep people happy, you have to stay humble and try to take every negative comment and turn it into something positive. Some customers may have the most irrational requests and problems which you may not even be able to solve. You should always try to be as understanding and respectful to your customers so new customers can relate to your business and see how important customers are to you, no matter how they treat you. While this may sound difficult to do at times, doing this creates a great impression on customers, and you tend to become a more reliable brand.

### *Self-promotion*

It's obvious why you are promoting your brand on Facebook but that doesn't mean you speak about your brand directly. Self-loathing and self-promotion can create a negative impact on your business. If you want to create a strong impression amongst people that you believe can be potential customers, you need to do it in a subtle manner and you have to get their attention. Self-promotion techniques are outdated and they don't work. Try not to directly sell your brand when you are promoting on Facebook. Try and incorporate a social message that will increase the feel good factor for your brand.

### *Spamming*

Just because you get personal information from your customers or your followers from Facebook does not mean you should spam them. All businesses should personally interact with their customers and consistently ask them if they are interested in the services that they have to offer. Sometimes people simply like your business because it's around their area and because it is close by when they need the type of services you offer. Not all potential customers who follow your business want to become customers instantly. You need to give customers time when they show interest in your business rather than pushing them.

## Too Little Interaction

The reason people follow your fan page on social media is that they want to get more information out of you. If you don't share enough on your Facebook page, it may create a bad impression on people and they will eventually get bored. A lot of people on Facebook tend to unfollow pages that are not active. If you don't want to be one of these pages, make sure you regularly update it.

## No Real Followers

Business owners believe it is a tough battle on the internet and in order for them to stay ahead of the competition they need to have more followers on social media than their competitors. This often leads to them purchasing fake followers from a number of companies that sell these followers online. It does not help your business because it gives followers the false impression that you have a strong social media page. These followers are just a number and they don't profit your business in any way. This is something that isn't going to get you any returns and is in no way going to strengthen your social media presence. Good things take time and even with followers, you need to be patient.

## Using Automated Systems and Depending on Them

There are various websites that allow you to automatically post to your social media pages. This is great for when you are on holiday and on days where you are not able to post on your own, but it's best not to make a habit out of it. The problem with these automated websites is that you tend to forget real interaction with your customers - your customers would like responses from you when they ask you questions. If you rely completely on automated systems, you won't be able to give them a timely response and this will lead to the downfall of your business.

## Seeming Monotonous

If you continuously post the same kind of content on your social media pages, specifically on Facebook, people will get bored. You need to experiment and post new things from time to time. The best thing about Facebook is that it gives you the opportunity of experimenting between text advertisements, image ads, and even video ads. Having this to your advantage, it's a good idea to make the most out of it.

## Sharing Irrelevant Content

You should share new content on a daily basis but that doesn't mean that you can just post about anything. What you share on social media has to be relevant to your business, which is why it's important to create content in that manner. When you share content that is irrelevant, it's not going to benefit your business.

## No Tracking

If you don't have an analytic tracking system on your Facebook page, you won't know what is happening and what kind of responses you are getting from the audience. This means that you are shooting in the dark without knowing what your goal is and whether or not you are actually achieving it.

## Using Multiple Profiles

A lot of times, business owners believe that they can ask various employees to create different business pages and promote them all at the same time. This is the biggest mistake that you can make as none of these pages will get the good following and customers will be confused to which the original one actually is. If you want to get the right kind of exposure on social media, you need to focus on one business page.

## Using Bad Language

This is simply a clear rule that all business owners should follow not only on social media but in any form of interaction with their customers. It's important to respect your customers and treat them in a formal manner. Using foul language or bad language, in any sense, is considered a violation of your business rules and something that you shouldn't do.

**Featuring Sex, Drugs or Violence on Your Page**

A lot of business owners believe that this is exactly what helps to sell products. But the truth is this only helps you to get a bad reputation in the market. What helps you sell your product is a good quality product and strong social media marketing skills. You don't need to use any negative methods to promote your business when you can do it the right way and do it effectively.

**Not Having a Dedicated Team**

If you want to get effective social media responses, you need to have experts who handle social media marketing in the right way. In order for you to do this, it always makes more sense to have a team dedicated to the job who can market your business effectively and do it without any mistakes.

# Creating Fun Social Media Posts

There is a lot that you can do in order to keep your social media page fun and engaging. But if you want to do something that attracts large amounts of followers and makes you an internet sensation overnight, it's important for you to think out of the box and do something innovative. The best part about marketing on Facebook is that you don't have to limit yourself to using only image-based or using only text-based advertisements to promote. Whether you want to share videos, an event, or an image, you can do it all. What you need to do is make sure the images or videos that you share are something that has the potential to go viral.

If you are not sure how to do this, you can always hire professional social media marketers who know how to get the right kind of advertisements to create awareness. All you need is one successful post for your business to become a known brand across the globe. Here are a few examples of Facebook advertisements that went viral.

### The Ice Bucket Challenge

The Ice Bucket Challenge was probably the most popular challenge across the world among people belonging to different age groups and ethnicities. When this began people saw a lot of celebrities attempting it. There was something about the Ice Bucket Challenge that pushed people to attempt it themselves. From children to people as old as sixty, they all attempted it, all posted videos, and made it go viral across the world. There were over 17 million videos across various countries that were uploaded and even some of the most popular celebrities such as Oprah Winfrey and Bill Gates also attempted to do the ice bucket challenge. The challenge was meant to raise funds and it successfully managed to raise over $220 million. This challenge was different, unique and it stood out amongst other social media posts. It was fun and challenging at the same time.

### Reverse Robbery

Reverse robbery was started off by a brand called OAK milk when they realized that the sales were dropping. Once the campaign hit Facebook, the sales shot up by 50% and there a sudden spike in the number of fans on their page as well. The reverse robbery campaign was very unique. The four masked men in the campaign would forcibly stock stores with oak milk. These stores were targeted based on polls conducted on Facebook.

### The Light Machine

This was one of the craziest gimmicks on social media that was done by Pepsi. The company created a vending machine that would give out a free can of Pepsi to anybody who liked their Facebook page. Needless to say, it took their sales through the roof and also increased their presence on social media. While it may have cost Pepsi a lot in terms of retail revenue, it was actually quite a cost-effective method to become popular. They went ahead with this without too much branding and still managed to get the kind of exposure they were looking for.

### Do Us A Favor

Lays had a rather unique concept of keeping people engaged on Facebook. It asked their fans to constantly share new flavors they would like to try out with their bag of chips. They also introduced a reward for the person who suggested the most successful flavor. Needless to say, the idea went crazy.

These were just a few examples of some of the most innovative methods of promoting business on social media. You don't have to have a big budget to do it. All you need to do is think in a creative manner and you are bound to come up with something that will get people's attention and go viral.

# Promote Your Facebook Business Page for Free

Not all businesses have a budget set aside for social media marketing. If you are a new business and you have a limited amount of money to spend, then advertising on social media might not be one of the priority expenses in your book. That doesn't mean that you can't create awareness on this platform. You can sign up on Facebook and you can also create your own fan page without having to spend any money. If you want to promote your Facebook page without any investments, here are some interesting ways you can do it.

### *Target Your Friends and Family*

When you are a small business, the best way to start is to send invitations to your friends and family asking them to like your page. Not only should you send an invitation to them but you should also send a message telling them a little about your business and interacting with them on a personal note. Do this with all the people on your Facebook list and try as much as possible to get them to share it with others as well. The more you interact with your friends and family, the higher the chance is that they will share your page and get more people to like it.

## Offer Promotions

Once you know you have a certain number of people following your page, start giving out some interesting offers. Ask people to share it and tell them that the more they share, the higher the chances of getting the offer. When you do this, make sure you are actually giving out something, even if it's a really small gift. It helps you to stay in your customers' good books and they will always look forward to contests in the future. When you have multiple people on your page, you begin earning money - sharing a part of your profit to increase sales is a smart approach to adapt.

## Provide the Right Content

When people follow your Facebook page, they want to get information regarding your business. You need to provide them with that kind of information but in an interesting and informative way. The last thing you want to do is have your Facebook fan page be boring. People usually scroll through their Facebook page until something interesting catches their eye. You should try and provide them with that kind of content so that they stay hooked.

### Share Positive Feedback

When you sell your first product or service to somebody, ask them to give you a rating and provide feedback on your fan page. Share the feedback with others so that they know you are worth their attention. It's difficult for a new business to establish a strong presence on Facebook, but with a little persistence and a lot of effort, you will eventually get there.

### Interact With and Keep Track of Influencers

There's nothing better than interacting with an influencer and having them to help you in promoting your Facebook page. While social media influencers charge money to do this, there's no harm in requesting them because you never know, they might just be in a really good mood and help you out this once.

### Updating Your Page

The last thing you need to remember is to keep your Facebook page up to date and provide all the information that customers look for. If you have a business website, make sure you update that as well and mention your working hours on your Facebook page. You can do all of this with no cash investment.

# Facebook Advertisements and Small Startups

It is easy for big brands to promote their businesses on Facebook because money isn't a problem for them. However, when you have just started out and you are cutting corners to try and save as much money as possible, spending a lot on Facebook advertisements might not seem like the best thing for you to do. If you are just starting out, you need to understand certain facts about Facebook marketing before you blindly put in your money.

## Facebook Advertisements are Expensive

It might seem worth it to you that $2 can get you about 20 followers on your fan page. But you need to remember that within these 20 followers, there might not be even one person who is interested in purchasing your service and that could mean that you are at a loss. Rather, you should invest your money to constantly run advertisements on Facebook. While these advertisements are not cheap, you will reap the rewards from it by getting genuine followers. You need to begin by testing out various advertisements to see what suits your business best.

## Generating Leads May Seem Lucrative

Leads mean potential customers and this was what excites a lot of startups. Startups begin to invest a lot of money to generate leads via Facebook. This might not be the best way to begin, especially if you don't have a lot of financing to support the advertisements on a regular basis.

You have to remember that once your promotion stops, your

leads stop coming. If you want this to be a constant rotation, you have to keep on putting in money and this will eventually drain out the business. This is because the money from your customers will take a longer time to come in as opposed to the money going into advertisements.

If you are promoting your business on Facebook and you have a limited budget, always start small. You need to put in more effort if you want to get the right responses and this effort should not cost you money. Facebook advertisements are great, but it works better when you have a certain number of followers because this helps you to get the right kind of exposure. It is always better to start without any investments and work your way to the top rather than begin promoting your business by spending money.

## Increase Facebook Engagement

Facebook is a user-friendly platform. Creating an account or a business page is very simple. The difficult part is promoting this page and getting the right kind of audience to constantly visit and like your services. There are various things you can do on Facebook that can prove to be beneficial and not all of these things require money. If you are looking for the best ways to engage the audience on Facebook then you need to understand what they are looking for. Here are some of the latest trends that Facebook business owners have observed which help them to increase their online presence.

# Posting the Right Amount of Times

Some business owners believe that they should update their Facebook page every 2 hours. Others believe they should post only once a day. You need to understand that people on Facebook do not look forward to seeing an overload of posts from you. Rather, they prefer to see one post that's really interesting. However, this doesn't mean that you should only post once, as most of the time all your customers are not going to see that one post that you have shared. The optimum number of times that you should share on Facebook is three times a day. This is because there are some people who tend to check their Facebook accounts in the morning, there are others who check it in the afternoon, and there are those who like to check it once they get home from work in the evening. If you share Facebook posts three times a day, you will reach all these people and there won't be repetitive content for them to see.

# Post When They Are Online

There are various ways to figure out what time you should share your Facebook posts but it is always recommended to share your posts anywhere between 7 am to 10 am because people who like to check their phone in the morning during these hours. Your second post should be shared anywhere between 12 pm to 2 pm during a typical lunch break, and the last should be shared anywhere between 5 pm 8 pm which is around the time most people return home.

## Create Advertisements Specifically for Facebook

Many business owners believe that they can share the same post on Instagram as well as Twitter. This is the biggest mistake you will make because posts that you share on different social media platforms will be viewed by people who follow you on multiple platforms. You need to give them something fresh and different so that they enjoy you on all of these platforms. While you may want to focus on Facebook, you should not lose out on the number of people who follow you on other platforms as well.

## Experiment with Videos

If you have a creative team with you, this is something that will definitely benefit your business. A recent survey showed that people on Facebook prefer watching videos as opposed to reading text on Facebook because they find it more interesting. All you need to do is come up with ways of sharing videos and you can watch them go viral in no time.

## Interact with People

One of the best ways to interact with people on social media, specifically on Facebook, is to ask them for their opinion. This may seem tricky because it's always frightening to know what customers really think about you, but it is also refreshing because you will learn more about your business and you will manage to rectify errors and make your business stronger. When you allow interaction, customers look forward to interacting as well and they will continue checking your page.

Facebook marketing is effective but also can cost a lot of money, which is why business owners cannot continue to spend on advertisements. If you want to make the most out of your advertisements, you need to do something creative to interact with the audience regularly and keep them hooked. If you manage to do this the right way, not only will you get repeat business from existing customers, you will also see more people liking your page as more existing customers share your information.

## Get Creative

There are some businesses that have a very refined audience and if your business is one of those, then interacting with your kind of customers could get tricky. For example, if you are a divorce lawyer, then the one thing that you would look for is for people who have recently changed their relationship status. If you are a moving company then you will need to keep an eye on people who are either planning to move or have mentioned about this on their Facebook page. This helps you to get more exposure without spending too much. This is called event tracking – a part of Facebook advertising that you can look into.

## Lookalike of The Existing Leads

Just because people have shown interest in your business and haven't become customers, it that does not mean they have no scope to become customers. Anybody who is on your Facebook page and has liked your business page is a potential customer and you need to treat them with just as much importance as you would treat a new customer or a new lead. These are also the people who will help you to share more information so when you put something exciting on your business page, you can expect them to share this information with their friends who probably fall into the same criteria as they do. They could be your potential customers as well.

This is called a lookalike audience, and it is also a part of the

Facebook advertising campaign.

Like any other method of advertisement, Facebook advertisement also involves a little experimentation, and you need to make sure that you test things out before you finally stick to something that works. Times change and people constantly look for new and different things. Once you establish your followers, you need to start increasing your number of followers without spending too much money. This can only be done when you promote your business in an effective way from the beginning. Look to create an impact that works in the benefit of your business.

## Instructions on How to Use the Facebook Ad Manager

Facebook is a user-friendly social media platform, but Facebook ads aren't as user-friendly as you would probably like it to be. If you have just started out with the Facebook ads manager, there are going to be a number of obstacles that will come your way. In order for you to be able to use Facebook ads manager to its full potential, you need to understand the functionality of the manager and figure out all its features effectively before you finally use it.

# Step-by-Step Guide to Create Facebook Advertisements

When you are on your Facebook page, scroll down from the dropdown menu on the upper right and click on 'create ads'. Facebook has an ad manager that will automatically open up and help you to figure out how to create your first advertisement. If you've never advertised on Facebook before using the ad manager, it is definitely something you may want to consider doing.

Once you open up the ad manager, you will see that there are various options that can help you design and create your own advertisement on Facebook. Make sure to look into all these options and understand them before you skip to the next step.

Save your most used tools in the 'frequently used' section to save time. These are the tools that you can continuously use to create various Facebook advertisements whenever you want without having to go through all the tools available on Facebook.

Once you have chosen the tools that you want and you are ready to go ahead with the advertisement, you can click on audience insight and decide how you want to filter the audience that views your ads. If you are a local business, then it makes more sense to select a geographic criterion of up to 5 km around your business location. While this may get you less exposure, it will get more effective exposure that matters to your business.

When you select a certain demographic, it consequently

exposes more details to you including age, gender and a lot more. It will also tell you about their activity, their purchases, and other information that you can use to your benefit. The longer time you spend on understanding these demographics, the better it is for your business. You can then move ahead to the 'create and manage' section where you will create an advertisement and also be able to manage it. If you have multiple advertisements running then there is a business manager that you can use to help you observe these advertisements. Business managers could be anybody from your organization who you can grant access to the tool.

There is an ads manager tool that you can use which can help you customize reports and download the various data that is relevant to the campaign for you to share with your team.

The power editor tool is a great tool that helps you design your advertisement more effectively and include content in the heading to save space.

The page post tool is an analytic tool that helps you to check the last post that you have shared and see how much exposure the post got. You can check the reach, as well as the actions that were taken on the post in order to figure out which post worked the best. This is one of those tools you should frequently use because it gives you a clear insight into the various campaigns you conducted and helps eliminate campaigns that were not as effective.

Automated rules is an important tool that you should always keep handy because it helps you set a certain limit for an advertisement and ensures that you don't go over budget on any given day.

# Measure and Report

Once you have a clear idea of what's going on with your Facebook ads, you can use that report to analyze what time works well for your advertisements and also which advertisements were more popular among the ones that you shared. It also helps you to figure out which of these advertisements help you to get visitors to your website. This is known as the custom conversion tool.

All of these tools that are available on Facebook ad manager are very simple to understand and they come with step-by-step instructions, making it even more convenient for you to use. All you need to do is pay attention to the text that is written on the advertisement tools so that you can put them to the best possible use.

Another section in the ads manager is something that can help you to figure out how to build your audience as well as advertisements based on what has worked well for you in the past. This is where your lookalike audience can come in handy. If you've already managed to target a certain audience, you can then try to clone the audience with a lookalike audience to get similar results. This helps you to save time and ensures that you don't go back to the same customers over and over again.

The settings tab is where you can personalize your account and also keep it secure. You can also update your payment information, your email account, and all the other details that you would like to display on this page. The ads manager may seem very difficult to understand in the beginning, however, once you look through the tools, you will realize that everything is segregated in an effective way for you to make the most out of them. This is a page you need to spend a lot of time on to get all the information that is important for your business. This is where you can determine how effective the ad was and what changes need to be made.

# How to Advertise More Effectively

We have already established that advertising on social media platforms can be extremely beneficial for your business. However, choosing the right kind of advertisement that will appeal to the audience can be difficult to figure out. As a business owner, one is bound to get overwhelmed by the ideas that they can choose from and then figuring out what the audience will like and what they would not like.

If you have the budget for it, try to use all forms of advertisement on Facebook as it will definitely work in your favor. This is because it will give you clear insights into what has worked and what you need to stop doing. If you are looking to start Facebook advertising then here are some interesting ways for you to capture your potential customers with the right kind of advertisements.

### 6 Tricks to Create ´Scroll-Stopping´ Photos on Facebook

Photos are the most popular way of promotion on Facebook. The only problem with sharing generic photographs is that people tend to scroll past and ignore what you have shared. If you want to make sure that they stop scrolling and look at the image that you have shared, then here are some interesting tips that will help you do this in a more effective way.

## *Stay On-Brand*

Consistency is really important - when you share an image on Facebook, you need to make sure that the image looks consistent to all the other images that you have shared in the past. While you can get as creative as you like with these images, you also need to make sure that there is a small logo of your brand on the image so people know that your business is sharing it. If you share interesting content and your logo is part of the content, the chances of potential customers stopping to look at the image increase considerably. This is because people relate with your brand and they will want to see what you have shared.

## *Know Your Size*

The size of the image that you share on social media platforms is important. If you share an image that's too large it gets difficult for people to look at the entire image especially when they are on their phones and will they tend to ignore it completely. When sharing on Facebook, make sure that you keep size in mind and that you keep all posted images at that consistent size.

## *Use Stock Images*

If you are on a tight budget and you don't want to spend a lot of money on a graphic designer to create images for you, there are plenty of free images that you can take advantage of. All you need to do is spend time researching where you can get the best images related to your business. Before sharing the image, ensure you add your brand name on the image, then you will be ready to share them.

**Take Your Own Photos**

You don't have to have a DSLR in order to take interesting pictures that you can share on your business page. Grab your smartphone and start capturing things you think are interesting and it will attract the right audience. This could be random pictures of your workplace, products that you are selling, or even something completely random that you find funny. The more you personalize images and the more you let people know about your business, the closer they get to your brand and end up associating themselves with you.

**Change Up Your Posts**

Instead of sharing the same kinds of images try to spruce things up by using different ones. This doesn't mean that you have to do a different sized image or something that is irrelevant to your brand. It simply means to share quotes sometimes, tips or even offer motivational images from time to time.

**GIFs**

If you don't want to share videos, you may want to consider sharing GIFs. These moving graphical images can help you to generate a lot of response. Just like you can get free photographs, you can also get free GIFs on various websites. Most of these are eye-catching and a lot of fun to share, as long as you manage to relate them to your business.

## 8 Tricks to Create 'Scroll-Stopping' Videos on Facebook

The minute Facebook allowed video-sharing, people went crazy. More and more businesses started using videos to their benefit and managed to attract a lot of followers on their business pages. If you've always been interested in the idea of sharing videos on your Facebook page but you are not too sure what's going to work, here are 7 tips and tricks that you should definitely try out.

### Upload Videos Directly to Facebook

Most business owners make the mistake of copying a link and sharing it on Facebook as a video as they don't know that they can upload a video directly to Facebook. The benefit of uploading a video directly to Facebook is that it is always going to be the right size and you will manage to upload it in a more effective way without posting links. When you upload a link instead of a video, some people go directly to the source and you could end up losing that potential customer because of it.

### Create a Strong Impression Within the First 4 Seconds

The first few seconds are the deciding factor on whether the audience is interested in viewing the video or if they just want to move on. You have to do something to impress the person watching the video within the first four seconds in order for them to stop scrolling. If they watch it for the first four seconds, they will likely watch the entire video - this is why you need experts to help you design good quality videos.

### Use Facebook 360

Facebook 360 allows you to take a virtual tour with the help of an image by giving you 360-degree coverage. Real estate agents can save a lot of time by simply showing a house online as opposed to having people go all the way to the location. If someone likes what they see in a panoramic Facebook 360 post they can then decide to go and pay a visit to the actual place.

### Add a Video to Your Page

It's important for you to feature videos on your fan page because these videos will help engage people to stay on your page for a longer time.

### Provide Information About the Video

A lot of times, business owners simply upload a video without giving out any information. While some people begin to watch a video almost instantaneously because it auto-plays, there are people who need to click on the play button to watch a video and they will not watch it unless they know what the video is about. While you don't have to give them all the details, you definitely need to give them some intrigue to make them watch the video.

### Add A Call-To-Action

Video sharing is fun and it definitely manages to get with the right kind of attraction, but your end goal is to make people come to your business page and buy products from you. The only way this is going to happen is when you have a strong call-to-action that encourages people to do it.

### Video Length

The optimal video length should not be more than three-minutes. The shorter, the better. If there is a lot of information you want to share, cut the video into multiple three minute videos.

### Don't Forget Sound

Most videos on Youtube are watched with the sound turned off on mobile phones or computers when a person is at work. When creating a video make sure it's just as interesting with the video off as it is when the volume is turned on.

## 4 Tips for Negative Feedback on Facebook and How To Deal with It

Even the best businesses end up with negative comments. It may be embarrassing because you are exposed in front of many people and you might not know what to do. If you've experienced this and you are not too sure how you should deal with it, then here are 4 tips that will help you understand how to deal with the situation effectively.

### Stay Positive

Sometimes negative comments can get really offensive and this could make you want to reply to them in a negative manner. You need to understand that it is important for you to stay positive and appreciate the comment anyway. If someone has a negative reaction towards a certain business idea that you've come up with, you may want to try and rectify it.

### Apologize When Needed

If somebody isn't happy with your product or service, feel free to ask them what went wrong and apologize for it going wrong. Apologizing to somebody lets people know you are open to suggestions.

## Don't Tick People Off

Sometimes businesses get backlash because of the kind of posts that they share. The best way to avoid this is to refrain from posting anything that is political or religious. Do not share anything that you would not otherwise send to another person because this will definitely annoy a few people.

## Look at the Comments as a Good Thing

When you have negative feedback, this simply means you are attracting people, both good and bad. A lot of people tend to read hateful comments in a positive light. If you are getting hate comments, don't be deterred by it. There are also going to be people who will view those comments positively and will stand by your business. Any kind of publicity is good publicity and when you are getting it for free, so make the most out of it.

# Chapter 7 - Instagram Marketing and Advertising

While marketing on Facebook is definitely the first choice for many people, it doesn't necessarily mean it's the best. For a few businesses, Instagram can work in a more effective way compared to Facebook. If you think you will manage to target more people on Instagram than you could on Facebook, then it's important for you to plan your marketing strategy in the right way.

Instagram is the second most popular social media app in the USA alone, and the numbers continue to increase. Not just in the USA, but all around the world people are getting more attached to Instagram because pictures tend to tell a better/more straightforward story. If you want to start your business promotions on Instagram, here are a few things that you should keep in mind.

## Set It Up the Right Way

Unlike Facebook that has detailed pages for all your information, Instagram has a very small bio section where you can add certain details about your business. You need to make your bio very strong so it creates a positive impact on people. It needs to include all the details of your business in a limited amount of words. You should also remember to add your business website and other social media handles where users can follow you.

## Stories are Great

Instagram has a feature where they tell users when somebody posts a story. It's a regular reminder on a daily basis so even if somebody misses your posts, they will definitely not miss your story. A story is something that you can share that stays on your page for 24 hours. Stories are interesting and you can do various things with it, including adding a short video along with multiple pictures at the same time. Something that tugs on the emotional strings of a viewer's heart always works well to gain more views.

## Check Out the Latest Trends

Similar to Facebook, when you promote on Instagram, it is always better for you to check out what's trending and how your competitors are creating traffic. This will give you a clear idea of what you need to do in order to increase your likes or followers on Instagram.

## Reply to Comments Regularly

Commenting works well on Instagram so make sure that you make it an integral part of your routine to reply to all the comments that you receive. Most retail businesses choose to indulge in Instagram because they can constantly share images of their new products. In order to keep the audience engaged, you need to ensure that you stay at the top of your game and reply to comments.

## Influencer Marketing

Influencer marketing works best on Instagram because it helps you to get more followers who are interested in your product. Always look for influencers who will relate to your product and will manage to promote it in a genuine way. There are various kinds of influencers that you can rope in - you don't have to necessarily look for someone who is a celebrity or a pop icon. Micro-influencers can help you create just as strong an impact, especially for small businesses.

## Get Familiar with Hashtags

Instagram is all about hashtags, so even if you miss promoting your product your followers will manage to track you if you use the right hashtags. It will take you a while to figure out these hashtags but once you do it, it becomes really easy to connect with the right kind of people.

When you use the right hashtags, you manage to generate more visitors to your Instagram page and these people eventually may visit your website as well. If you are into e-commerce, Instagram is perfect for you because you can simply include a 'buy now' link for all the products that you share. Instagram is very easy to understand and it's more convenient to use in comparison to Facebook which requires a lot of research and understanding before you reap maximum benefits out of it. Once you understand how to use Instagram, you will manage to grow your follower count in a short time span.

## Influencers vs Paid Advertisements vs Non-Paid Promotions

One of the most popular ways to promote your business on Instagram is to get the assistance of an influencer. Business owners are always confused in regards to how much working with an influencer really costs and how they can rope one in. There are various factors that you need to take into consideration when getting in touch with an influencer.

If you are a local business, then choosing a micro-influencer who is popular in the locality, is likely to be a better solution for you in comparison to a popular one who will charge you more money. Micro-influencers tend to be cheaper in comparison to bigger ones and could charge anywhere between $250 to $1000 dollars per post.

Advertisers, on the other hand, turn out to be a little cheaper.

The difference between choosing an influencer versus an advertiser is that an influencer will get you more exposure in areas that matter and while you may pay more, you also get branding for your business, which can't be done simply with the help of marketing.

Non-paid methods of promotion are also great, but they need to be done in an effective way and it may take a lot of time to get your brand established if you opt for this method. Influencers usually bring a higher engagement rate compared to advertisements which is why they have become more popular. However, depending on the nature of your business you need to decide whether an influencer will work well or whether you want to choose advertisements on Instagram instead.

Retail businesses can benefit the most from influencers because they can help establish a brand for the business overnight. Service-related businesses can also benefit from influencers but in this industry, an advertisement can also pay off. Similar to Facebook, Instagram also offers various filters that you can use in order to choose the right kind of audience you would like the advertisement to be visible to.

If you are a makeup brand and you want to make a big name for your product in the market almost instantly, then the best way to do it would be to get in touch with an influencer who shares a lot of makeup tips. Simply asking them to promote your product on one of their blog posts can turn tables and can help shoot up your sales instantly.

Offering deals on these makeup products can also help you to get a lot of sales but it won't be as effective as it would be with the help of an influencer. You need to think about the pros and cons that come with either of the branding methods and decide what you think will suit your business the best. When you choose an influencer, you also need to have a certain amount of money kept aside to pay the influencer in order to market your product regularly.

## Instagram Videos & Photos vs Facebook Videos & Photos

Sharing a video on Instagram is a little more complicated compared to Facebook because of the time constraints that Instagram has. In regard to photographs, it is more convenient for you to share as many as possible on Instagram without having to struggle too much in order to create an album or decide where you want to upload the pictures.

One of the best things about sharing on Instagram is that you can also share them on Facebook by simply selecting the 'Share on Facebook and Twitter' option. This is something you can't do when you are on Facebook. Instagram also has the option of telling a story and this is great especially if there's something exciting happening with your business or there is something you want people to know about but don't want it to stay on your page permanently.

When you share videos on Instagram, you can choose to either add it to your story or post it as a complete video. With videos, it is always better to share them on your page because you get a longer time frame. With images, it is something you can always decide depending on whether it is something you would like to have permanently on your page or if it's something that you could delete after being seen. You also need to make sure you caption your videos. Viewers should be able to know what's going on even when the sound is turned off.

Do not have too many Instagram stories at one time because it becomes difficult for people to scroll through all of them and they eventually forget what the content of your story was. If you want your story to create an impact, make sure that the story is concise so it gives out all the details and people remember it.

## Ideal Length of Instagram Videos

Instagram videos are a lot shorter in comparison to the videos you share on Facebook. There have been many speculations that Instagram is increasing the duration of videos you can upload, but as of today the maximum length of a video that you can share on Instagram is 60 seconds. Although Instagram videos are shorter in length, they always manage to create a huge impact. Another great thing about Instagram videos is that you can share multiple videos in a single frame. This makes it interesting for people to view.

If you are sharing an Instagram video on your story, this video needs to be no more than 15 seconds. As opposed to an Instagram video on your page, Instagram stories should be one video at a time rather than multiple videos as these tend to work better.

Videos can communicate a lot about your business and it also helps people relate to the brand more effectively. When creating videos, you don't have to have a professionally designed one. It can be anything from a simple video about the functionality of a product to a service that was successfully completed or even a testimonial of a satisfied customer talking about the business. You should always try new things with videos so you keep people entertained and you have new information to share as well.

## 3 Tricks to Create 'Scroll-Stopping' Photos on Instagram

There is no denying that when it comes to sharing pictures, there is no better place for you to share it than Instagram. Whether you want to share images for your business or whether you want to share it to sell a product, it is always more beneficial to do it the right way.

### Share Clear Images

One of the major benefits of using Instagram is that you can share images of different sizes and it automatically resizes it for you. Instagram is highly effective because of a number of filters that you can use to your advantage. Even if your picture isn't as clear as you want it to be, you can always try out a new filter that can help bring out the best of the picture.

### Don't Only Use Hashtags

Hashtags are a great way to locate an image but it is also important for you to make sure you let people know a little about the image by writing a few lines. This works well in your favor and people will always be interested to read what you've written.

## *Publicize Your Brand*

Every image that you share should have something to do with your brand or even just include a small logo at the bottom corner of the image to let people know that your brand is active on Instagram. Even if the pictures have nothing in common with each other, make sure to connect them in some way or the other by simply adding your brand logo on them.

## *3 Tricks to Create´Scroll-Stopping´ Videos on Instagram*

The duration of an Instagram video might not be long, but that doesn't necessarily mean it won't have an impact on your business in a positive way. Instagram videos are just as effective as Facebook videos and if you want to make sure that you make the most out of sharing videos then here are some effective tips for you to keep in mind.

### *Learn About the Culture*

Instagram is trendy, and unlike Facebook, there are various trends that keep changing. Keep yourself updated as much as possible with the trends so that you can incorporate them into your videos and get people to watch them.

### *Share Interesting Videos*

You can't expect to share any sort of content and get the right kind of hits that you are expecting. The videos you share should be worth watching and you should have invested a certain amount of time in creating it. Even if you choose to share a video that doesn't belong to you, make sure the video has some sort of message and is related in some way to your business. The best way to make your videos go viral is to post two sets of videos and test them against each other to see which one does better.

## Use Analytics

When you share videos on Instagram, make sure to check the analytics from time to time. This will help you understand which videos did well and which ones didn't. After a little experimenting, you will manage to figure out which videos are the kinds of videos you should share and which are the ones you need to keep away.

## 3 Tips to Create a Highly Converting Ad

Advertising on Instagram has become quite a trend and a lot of business owners are investing time in getting this done. If you would like to make the most of Instagram advertising then here are three tips that will help your advertisement give you better returns. You can also test a couple of advertisements against each other to see which ones work well and stick to the ones that perform better than the rest.

## Promote Good Content

When you pay for an advertisement, make sure that you pay for the best work that you can share and ensure that you get it created and looking aesthetically pleasing. Instagram is all about pictures, so if your picture is a good quality one, there are chances that the returns on the pictures are going to be higher.

### *Filter the Audience*

Like with Facebook, take your time to filter the audience based on your business preference and geographic location. There are various other filters on Instagram as well that you can use to your advantage. Make sure to check them all and see which ones tick your boxes.

### *Promote in a Subtle Manner*

When you share a paid advertisement on Instagram, do not make it look like a direct advertisement but rather something people will be interested in. If you want people to purchase a product, you don't have to say, 'buy now' on the image. You can simply share a few pictures of the product and subtly place the 'buy now' link in the info that you place below the image.

Lastly, like Facebook, you are sure to face negative comments on Instagram as well. To deal with the negativity on Instagram, simply refer to the "How you should deal with negative comments on Facebook" section and apply the same theories on Instagram as well.

## Mistakes Beginners Make While Advertising on Instagram

Posting on Instagram is very effective as long as it is done the right way. In order for you to make the most out of your Instagram activities, you need to avoid mistakes common amongst beginners. Here are some of the most common mistakes that you need to avoid.

### Using Too Many Hashtags

This is one of the biggest mistakes that beginners make because they believe that the more hashtags they add, the more promotion it will do for their page. This is wrong and you need to understand that all you need is about 3 or 4 hashtags in order for you to promote your Instagram post effectively. Not only do lesser hashtags read better, but it also makes it easier for people to understand what you are trying to say.

### Do Not Automate Posts

This is the most common mistake that business owners make because they believe it will help them to save time. Once you begin automating posts on Instagram, you tend to forget signing into your account on a regular basis and you leave comments and queries unanswered.

### Don't Be Boring

The worst thing you can do on Instagram is to be boring. When you share something on Instagram, make sure it's interesting and innovative. Adding a worthless hashtag is something that makes no sense if it isn't on something worth sharing.

### Picking the Right Influencer

Business owners tend to spend a lot of money on influencers that seem to be really popular. You don't need to look for an influencer who is popular. You need to look for one who relates to your brand in the most effective way.

# Chapter 8 - YouTube Marketing and Advertising

In addition to Facebook and Instagram, YouTube marketing has also gained a lot of popularity. There are various businesses that prefer to share videos in order to enhance marketing efforts, and the best way to share these videos is by sharing them on YouTube. The reason YouTube marketing is more effective when it comes to videos is that you can rest assure someone has watched your video when it's placed at the start as opposed to when the ad is placed in between a video that they are watching.

YouTube is responsible for creating a lot of awareness for various businesses and it also works really effectively when you are a startup. If you have little or no credibility and you want to create mass awareness in a short time span, YouTube is probably your best bet.

YouTube belongs to Google – a company that has taken up most of the market today. With over a billion registered subscribers, people spend hours on YouTube each day watching videos across various genres.

No matter what kind of videos you are looking for, you are sure to find them on YouTube. This gives you leverage to add your advertisement to videos that are related to your business in some way or the other. When it comes to behavioral targeting, it is very effective to do it when you are doing it through YouTube. This is because you will find videos of all genres here and you will be able to relate your business to one of these genres.

## YouTube Marketing Strategies

Promoting your business on YouTube is great, but like all social media platforms, you need to begin with a strategy in mind. Without a strong strategy, your efforts on YouTube will go down the drain. There are various goals people have when they advertise on YouTube and it depends on the nature of your business. If you are a personality or a public figure, the only reason you'll advertise on YouTube is to get more visibility, if you are a business and you want people to come visit your website then that needs to be your goal. There are also e-Commerce websites that would like to sell products and these videos could simply include a 'buy now' link that directs a potential customer straight to their sales page to help increase sales. Your strategy needs to be based on your end goal and why you are advertising on YouTube in the first place.

## Kinds of Videos You Can Create on YouTube

YouTube is a video sharing platform so there is no limit to the length of a video that you can upload here. If you are creating videos that you would like to market on YouTube, you need to make sure you create them in an effective way so that it appeals to the mass audience. While YouTube is great to share videos, you need to remember there's a lot of competition on the platform and your videos have to stand out. If you want to create brand awareness for your business then make sure that the videos you put your focus on these points.

- Focus on the main core value of your business and talk about the various products or services the business deals with.

- Educate people on how to use these products or services.

- Use animated videos that are promotional for your products or services.

- Post customer reviews or documentaries about success stories with your products.

- Post interviews with influencers that can help increase brand value.

Unlike Facebook and Instagram, there aren't too many tools that are available for YouTube management. This is actually a good thing because it's simple. Managing your YouTube channel is very easy and it doesn't take as much time to figure it out in comparison to the other ad manager tools that are available on social media platforms.

This doesn't mean that you do not focus on the core necessity of promotion. It's just that all you can do on YouTube is share videos, and this is why it is a hassle-free service. There are a number of tools you can add to the social media management platform which can help enhance your advertisement in some way.

# Tools for Video Content

Apart from using these tools to incorporate your advertisement, you can also use a number of tools to help create the actual videos. These tools work well in enhancing your marketing efforts and they can add information that you would like to keep consistent in all your videos. If you are not too sure what kind of tools you can use, here are some that have proven to be really effective.

- Slidely Promo - This tool is particularly beneficial for live action videos.

- Wave - This tool can help you create videos to share on multiple social media platforms and repurpose your video content.

- Vyond – For if you are looking for an easy-to-use animated video to send.

# Tips for Increasing Subscribers and Views

At the end of the day, your main goal on YouTube would be to increase subscribers and views. This is how you can do it:

Promote your YouTube channel on various social media networks - once you have created a YouTube channel, you need to promote it in as many places as possible and this includes multiple social media pages. Try sharing your videos on these pages from time to time to increase the visibility of your YouTube channel.

Engage fans - Once you know that you have a certain number of subscribers, make sure you have them engaged in the various activities and videos you share by increasing your connection and interaction with them. Try to involve them in the brand in some way and get them to associate with your videos so that they feel that they are a part of something.

Add a YouTube widget to your blog - This simple button can automatically guide visitors on your website, blog, or YouTube channel so they can check out what is happening on the channel.

Contact other business owners to share videos - Get in touch with other business owners who have a YouTube channel and discuss and exchange videos with them. This helps you to promote each other's business and increase followers on each platform.

## Increase Traffic to Your YouTube Videos

Once you've increased the number of subscribers on your YouTube channel, you then need to start thinking about driving more traffic to the channel. There is a lot that you can do in order to attract more subscribers and increase traffic but here are a few foolproof methods that you definitely need to incorporate in your YouTube channel to get more visitors:

## Use Rich Keywords in the Video Tags

A lot of times business owners forget the importance of keywords when it comes to a video. You need to understand that irrespective of what kind of post you share, keywords matter. Without the right set of keywords, you will never manage to create a strong impression on the internet.

## Transcribe Your Videos

Transcription of your video helps in SEO efforts to a great extent. Sometimes people may not use the exact keyword that was listed but they may enter words that are mentioned in your video. If you transcribe the video and post it at the end of the video description, the chances that your video pops up in the search is always higher.

## Reply to Videos

If you notice that a video has a lot of heat and it is gaining a lot of popularity, the smart thing for you to do would be to go and comment on that video with your YouTube link. When you do this, you should keep in mind that you can't keep on going to multiple videos and placing your link because that's considered spamming. Do it just once on a specific video that relates to the content of your channel.

### Keywords in the Title of Your Video

The keywords that you choose don't just have to be in the description and in the body of the video, it also needs to be a part of the title. Titles are really important so take time to choose a quality title and don't use broken keywords.

### Insert a Video at The End of Your Video

This has become a popular trend with a lot of YouTubers these days. When you insert another video link at the end of your video, the chances that people will watch that video automatically increases and you get more traffic on your channel.

If you are looking to create highly effective advertisements on YouTube, you need to keep in mind the exact things that you do for Facebook and Instagram. What works on one social media platform could probably work on another, and in the sense of YouTube, it is a hassle-free way to promote your business as effectively as possible.

# Chapter 9 - LinkedIn Marketing

LinkedIn is a professional social media platform that all businesses register on. When it comes to hunting for professionals and checking out what is happening in the business world, LinkedIn is the place to be. As a business owner, promoting your services or products on LinkedIn should be one of your top priorities. If the class of people you are targeting are high-end business entrepreneurs, top management employees and people who take their work seriously, you are sure to find them on LinkedIn.

Promoting your business on LinkedIn is just like promoting it on any other social media platform. Based on a recent survey, it's proven that people with a higher income per annum choose to use LinkedIn more in comparison to other social media platforms like Facebook and Twitter. If you mean business, you have to stay on LinkedIn. LinkedIn is a little more professional, so you need to polish your skills as well as your marketing techniques.

While you can joke on Facebook and share a funny video, that's not what you want to do on LinkedIn. Most people on LinkedIn mean business and when they are on the platform, they aren't looking for any sort of entertainment. When you post an advertisement on LinkedIn, it needs to be clear, precise, and to the point. Leave the dramatic posts for Facebook and Instagram - LinkedIn has a serious tone.

One of the major things you need to focus on once you create a profile on LinkedIn is to ensure that it is one hundred percent complete. People on LinkedIn are very particular and they like to get all the information about you before they choose your business services or even before associating with you. In all probability, one of the major reasons that someone chooses to avoid your request to connect is because your profile is incomplete. Take the time to fill out all the details on LinkedIn so you make a lasting impression.

LinkedIn provides you with a number of connections as a suggestion and these are people you probably know already. The best way to increase your circle is to start out with these people because they will then refer you to other people in their circle and that's how your connections will increase. There are a number of groups on LinkedIn just like there are on Facebook. The more targeted groups you join, the more effective it is for your marketing efforts. The best part about LinkedIn is that even if you don't spend money to promote your business and you do the right things, you will manage to get the kind of visibility you seek and it helps to create a huge impact on your business.

## The Pros and Cons of LinkedIn Marketing

If you are planning to promote your business on LinkedIn, it's important for you to take into consideration the pros and cons of this social media platform. While it is an amazing place to promote your business, it is important that you choose the right decisions and the right methods of promotion so you benefit from it greatly.

*Pros*

- LinkedIn is an evolved social media platform that grants you complete access only after paying a certain fee. This indicates that people on the platform are serious about what they do and they are interested in career-oriented as well as business-related opportunities.

- It is consistent and you are very unlikely to find controversial issues that take place on LinkedIn.

- There are higher chances of connecting with more people on LinkedIn in comparison to other platforms, and an acquaintance will be more accountable associating with you on LinkedIn as compared to any other social media platform.

- You can get more information on LinkedIn about a person without actually connecting with them unlike any other platform.

- This is a professional environment and everything here is formal. There is almost no space for negativity.

- It is the fastest way for you to grow connections, considering the professional environment on LinkedIn.

*Cons*

- The age group on LinkedIn as little older in comparison to the other platforms so if your business is for people who are in a younger age group, you might not be able to find them here.

- LinkedIn is more expensive in comparison to other platforms and even if you just want to stay on the platform without any limits, you still have to pay.

- LinkedIn is very strict about what you post and most of the things you share will go through screening before it comes up on your wall.

- LinkedIn has a character limit, where you are allowed to post messages that are no longer than 600 characters.

## The Pros & Cons of Using Video on LinkedIn

Since LinkedIn is a professional social network, it becomes very convenient for businesses to connect on a professional level with others and share more information. Video sharing on LinkedIn is extremely beneficial - here are a few pros and cons of this new feature LinkedIn has just introduced.

**Pros**

- LinkedIn is the only network that targets the B2B market and it helps them to promote more effectively.

- It opens doors for product launches. There are various

company videos, information on DIY, webinars, and Q & A sessions which are taken more seriously on this platform.

- It's a great place for business owners to plan more professional interactions in a comfortable way.

- You can monitor the various analytics in regards to how many people have viewed and shared your video and you can get complete insights as well.

## *Cons*

- LinkedIn allows you to create videos that are more than 10 minutes in length but it's difficult for somebody to pay attention to such a long video. At most, you should focus on creating a video that is no longer than 3 minutes in length.

- The problem with videos is that it is difficult to open them in a workplace environment, considering the volume and the ability to view it or not.

- With the introduction of the video feature, LinkedIn has become a more casual zone and there is less control of content that is posted on the site.

# Tips for Attracting Followers on LinkedIn

Engaging people on LinkedIn is a little different in comparison to other social media platforms - it's always more professional. If you have been wondering what you can do in order to get more followers on LinkedIn, then here are some of the most effective ways to do this:

### Create Compelling Titles for Articles

One of the major areas that you need to focus on is creating good quality titles that will drive more people to your business page. The best way to do this is to do a lot of keyword research and ensure you choose a title that relates to your business and can help people learn more about it by simply reading the title. Your titles should be interesting and should want people to read on and see what it's all about. The key is to balance out between generating curiosity and providing a little information – both at the same time.

### Engage Your Employees

You need to encourage as many employees as possible to start following your business page because this will help to increase more followers organically without having to spend on the service.

### Promote a Page Outside of The Company

If you are spending on promotions, make sure you do it outside of the company so you don't waste resources on advertising to people who already know about your business.

### Engagement LinkedIn Groups

One of the most important things you should consider doing is to stay engaged in LinkedIn groups. This can help you to connect with as many people as possible who are related to your business and you can reap maximum benefits out of it.

### Launch a Follow Ad Campaign

A follow ad campaign is something that has a direct 'call-to-action' for people interested in your business or services. The message in this advertisement should be clear and it should let people know what they need to do once they see the advertisement. This is also what could be referred to as your end goal.

# Mistakes That Are Killing Your LinkedIn Profile

Your LinkedIn profile speaks volumes for your business and if you want your business to grow and become successful, it is important for you to create a strong profile. People end up spending a lot of money promoting their business but they soon realize they are not getting the kind of exposure that they seek. If you have been on LinkedIn for a while and you realize that you are not getting the response you expected, then here are a few reasons why this could be happening:

## A Bad Photograph

LinkedIn is a professional platform so the photograph that you use on LinkedIn needs to be professional.

## Inconsistent or Incomplete Headline

People want to know what you are doing and this is the reason your headline cannot be inconsistent or incomplete.

## An Incomplete Profile

When you are on LinkedIn, the one thing you should remember is to have a profile that is complete. Incomplete profiles do not get the kind of response that people expect.

## No Recommendations

When you are on LinkedIn, it's important for you to seek recommendations. The best way to do this is to reach out to the people who have been associated with your business. This could be a past association or a current one.

Apart from these major mistakes, people who tend to spam or provide unrelated information on the platform are also the kind of people that don't get right kind of exposure and cannot benefit from their LinkedIn profile.

# Chapter 10 - Other Marketing Channels

Apart from the mainstream social media platforms which people use on a regular basis to promote their businesses, there are also other alternatives you could try out. Some of these platforms may seem to be really effective and they can benefit you in a number of ways, as long as you put them to the right use. Twitter for one, has been on and off as a popular social media platform and if you use Twitter the right way, you can still increase your brand visibility quite effectively. Google Plus, Pinterest, and Snapchat are also other alternatives you could try out.

## Twitter

There has been a lot of speculation with regards to whether or not Twitter is a great place to market your business. There are a number of users who have stopped using Twitter completely because of the other alternatives available.

That being said, Twitter still has over 313 million active followers and contributors on the platform regularly. This makes it a great place for you to advertise your business specifically with small- and medium-sized businesses. The interaction on Twitter has been increasing since last year and it's really a great place to market your business.

# Snapchat

Snapchat is the youngest of the social media networks that are becoming popular. If your business is related to the young generation then Snapchat is probably your best bet. While this social media network doesn't work as well with the older crowd, it is something that is perfect to target those 19 and under.

# Pinterest

Long before Instagram became the most popular image sharing social media network on the planet, Pinterest existed. Although it has taken a backseat thanks to Instagram's popularity, Pinterest is still a viable option for you to share amazing pictures related to your business in order for you to get more popularity. The best part about Pinterest is that it can connect images with each other so the more images you share, the better it is for your business to get exposure when it's needed the most.

# Blogging And SEO

Irrespective of how many new trends come out and help your marketing efforts pay off, the one thing that remains constant throughout all online marketing strategies is the use of SEO efforts. The right kind of SEO will give you tremendous exposure and this can only be done with the right kind of blogging tools. While social media exposure is important, it's just as important for you to create a strong blog and have a good set of keywords to back it up. This is something that's going to remain an integral part of your business and it is also where you get to explain the details of your services or product and talk about them in a positive manner.

# Section 3: Monetizing and Growing Your Personal Brand

# Chapter 11 – Building An Email List

Once you start getting the right kind of exposure on social media platforms, your followers and subscribers automatically increase. The biggest mistake business owners make is believing that this is great for their business and they can now promote their services and products directly on these platforms. While it is important for you to stay active on social media network, it is important for you to create an email list that you can use to contact the leads you generate on a regular basis. This data usually includes your existing customers, potential customers, and people who are interested in your services or live in the area and could be future customers.

It is important for you to understand that all the followers and subscribers across various networking platforms including Facebook, YouTube, LinkedIn, and Instagram, are not owned by you. If some reason any of these platforms decide that they would like to shut down your account, you instantly lose all of those subscribers and everything that you worked for.

You are then left with the option of having to start over again and this means a big waste of time and resources.

It is important for you to understand that when you build an email list, it is something that you own. This list can be used to promote your business and also talk about the various services and discounts that you offer from time to time. Just like with titles on articles, you've got to keep the email titles hip and trendy. When picking a title for an email make sure it's not too long and it can be read on a mobile too.

While staying active on social media can help in establishing a brand, it is the email marketing efforts that eventually help to transform your brand into a big name and brings in more money for the business.

## Using Lead Magnets to Your Advantage

Capturing leads is usually the primary motive for any business. Irrespective of how old or young the business is, capturing new leads is the primary focus and this very rarely changes. These leads can help a business gain new customers and even expand their products and services based on feedback from these leads. However, getting good quality and valid leads is something that is not that easy to procure. Thankfully, with the help of lead magnets, you can now get high quality leads almost on a daily basis.

A lead magnet is nothing but an incentive that you offer a visitor in exchange for their email address or personal information. People are usually very skeptical when it comes to giving out their personal email. However, a lead magnet will usually have a very tempting proposition for them and they will be compelled to give up their personal information. For example, if you are a blog that talks about business strategies, your lead magnet could be a free book regarding the best business strategies from an industry expert. This will surely compel the visitor to give out their email address in order to receive the free book.

## Send Leads Through a Sales Funnel

Once the leads have been collected, you need to pass them through a sales funnel. Without a sales funnel, you will never know which lead can be a potential customer and which ones to discard. Lead generation is the process of converting customer awareness and then converting that awareness into a sale. With a good sales funnel, you will be able to gradually move your potential customer towards becoming a customer. For this, you need to build a relationship of trust with the lead. This may take days or even months, however; it needs to be done in the right manner, which is to provide correct information and tips that come in handy.

# Chapter 12 - Growth and Monetization

The beginning of a journey to create your social media page usually has a lot of ups and downs. But once you've reached your desired amount of followers, it's important for you to maintain and constantly aim at increasing the number of followers to create more awareness about your business while maintaining a strong relationship with your current customers.

You also need to learn how to grow and monetize your social media page as at the end of the day every business aims at earning revenue out of all the activities that they partake in. In order for you to monetize your efforts on social media, you need to play smart. The key is tricking people into thinking that you are not trying to sell them anything. Try to put across your brand message and subtly pitch in with a sale. For example, you are a business that sells pain relief spray. Try to show a video that shows a child getting injured and someone spraying the pain relief spray on the wound. Your punch line should be the sales pitch. Make people relate to the incident and how it could have been avoided with the help of your product.

Sharing content is important as the kind of content you share on social media proves whether or not you will manage to achieve your goal. Once you post on social media, you need to make sure that you get engagement from your followers and subscribers. In order for you to do this, you have to have a strong 'call-to-action'. While you don't have to directly promote products, you need to subtly hint at the promotion and ask people to check it out or figure out how to buy it.

You can also try to include offers from time to time which look lucrative and are irresistible to share. There are different things you can experiment with. The more shareable content you create, the more the likelihood of your followers increasing as well as your sales increasing is.

If you are a small business owner, you may want to consider trying to connect with bigger businesses that belong to the same industry as you. Getting them to recommend your services or even sharing a link, can have a huge impact on your business. Although some people believe that a big business will not pay attention to a small business, the truth is big businesses always look to do something nice for the community especially if it's a small business just starting out. Helping them to establish a reputation in the market and give them goodwill points will help big businesses as well.

## Ways to Make Your Content Marketing Go Viral

There is a lot that you can do in order to make a post go viral. Sometimes the least expected post goes crazy on the internet and you will surprise yourself. One of the things you need to keep in mind when aiming at creating a post is to make sure that the posts are innovative and unique. Something that you haven't shared before has a stronger chance of becoming popular on the internet in comparison to something that's already been shared. Here are a few things that you should consider when creating content you want to go viral:

- Keep it short as people don't like to spend a lot of time on any sort of advertisement.

- Make it genuine because at the end of the day it has to be something relevant and something that holds value and is true.

- Try to be interactive where you can by connecting with users and asking them for an opinion.

- And lastly, creating a compelling headline which can draw attention towards the post irrespective of its content.

## Study Influencers

Influencers will benefit your business in a great way. If you are wondering what you need to do in order to improve the popularity of your business, you need to observe an influencer and get handy tips from them. Here are a few things you should keep in mind.

- Document what goals you have and see what influencers do in order to perform, based on those goals.

- Observe their every move and make sure you take note of the various activities that they indulge in.

- Research multiple influencers at once so that you get as much information as you can.

- Build relationships with influencers as much as possible because this will help you to get closer to them and learn more about effective social media marketing techniques.

- Target micro-influencers if you have a limited budget. It is easier to deal with micro-influencers because they are not as popular and consequently have time to spare. They also connect with you better because they could be from the same locality and it makes more sense for you to ask them to assist you as compared to try and get a large influencer.

## Tips on Monetizing Your Personal Brand

If you are an entrepreneur or a startup and you're looking to monetize your personal brand, it's important for you to take as much advantage of social media as possible. Here are a few tips that can come in handy when you are establishing a personal brand:

- Research about various branding methods and learn from your competitors what works best. You can also get some handy tips from an influencer whose promoted products are similar to yours.

- Build on a strategy and work your way around it - strategies will pay off and you will manage to achieve your goals more effectively with a strategy than with an inconsistent plan. Monitor progress because if something goes wrong, you'll know you need to change it and you will be able to figure out mistakes a lot faster without it hampering your performance.

- Develop a brand and stick to it. Ensure that all the posts you share relate to your brand. Do not have inconsistencies when relating to your brand because this often confuses readers. If you want somebody to believe that your personal brand is popular, you have to constantly promote it.

- Communicate with the public on a regular basis and always stay responsive irrespective of how small or silly you think a query is. When you are open to responding, it creates a better impression and this helps people to stay loyal to your brand and take the first step towards becoming part of the brand as well.

## What Not to Do If You Want to Monetize Your Personal Brand

There is a lot of information that you can use to your benefit while establishing a personal brand on social media but it often gets confusing figuring out what you need to avoid. One of the main things you need to remember when promoting your personal brand is to stop aggressive self-promotion. Directly asking people to come and purchase products is not going to work because this creates a negative impact and you will eventually lose followers. You need to remember that the reason people end up following you on social media is because they like what you are doing and what you share. When you shift your focus towards direct promotions, it's not going to benefit anyone and you'll end up losing those followers.

If you stay inactive on social media for a really long time you will start to lose subscribers. It is a competitive world out there and the more active you are on social media, the stronger the chances your followers will remain loyal. Your behavior on your social media platforms is transparent so the last thing you want is to speak ill of a post or a negative comment. This is the kind of behavior that will definitely irk your followers. When you try to put down a competitor, it does not bode well for your business. This has to be consistent with all social media platforms. You should also remember the better your content is and the more positive your feedback is, the stronger the chances your subscribers will stay with you.

# Conclusion

Most business owners tend to get intimidated by the idea of social media marketing because the concept is so vast and there is so much that one needs to figure out. In order for you to gain success on social media, all you need to do is follow the right steps and not aim too high from the start. You need to constantly remind yourself that good things take time and if you want to have a large following on multiple social media platforms, you need to focus on the right things rather than purchasing them.

With everything available on the internet and platforms being so transparent, your efforts will be noticed. It's all about focusing and pushing towards success in order to gain popularity. With social media, you need to understand that once you become a big brand there is no turning back. The journey is a tough one and it needs to be a cautious one as well. Choosing the right decisions within social media marketing is something you need to do in order for your business and for you to achieve the end goal. Success isn't going to come to you overnight. It will eventually come once you start putting your social media efforts in the right place.

Technology has gotten the better of us and for some business owners it may be tough to transition from a completely offline business to something that is online and in full view of the public. Instead of letting this hinder you, you should make the most of it and begin to shine on the internet and take your business forward.

Social media marketing is all about getting out there and being social. There is no need to shy away from the people who can increase revenue and help your business grow and become successful! Approach them in the right manner and you'll never regret your decision. If you make the right decisions and ensure that your social marketing channels are handled well, you will have no problem getting your brand out there. While handling a social media account may seem easy as an individual, as an entity there are a number of factors that need to be looked into. You need to find the right balance between over posting and not posting at all.

Made in the USA
Coppell, TX
02 December 2019